The

YES/
NO

Book

The
YES/
NO
Book

HOW TO DO LESS...
AND ACHIEVE MORE

MIKE CLAYTON

PEARSON

Harlow, England • London • New York • Boston • San Francisco • Toronto • Sydney
Auckland • Singapore • Hong Kong • Tokyo • Seoul • Taipei • New Delhi
Cape Town • São Paulo • Mexico City • Madrid • Amsterdam • Munich • Paris • Milan

PEARSON EDUCATION LIMITED
Edinburgh Gate
Harlow CM20 2JE
United Kingdom
Tel: +44 (0)1279 623623
Fax: +44 (0)1279 431059
Web: www.pearson.com/uk

First published 2012 (print and electronic)

© Pearson Education Limited 2012 (print and electronic)

The right of Mike Clayton to be identified as author of this work has been asserted by him in accordance with the Copyright, Designs and Patents Act 1988.

Pearson Education is not responsible for the content of third-party internet sites.

ISBN: 978-0-273-77240-8 (print)
978-0-273-78149-3 (PDF)
978-0-273-78148-6 (ePub)

British Library Cataloguing-in-Publication Data
A catalogue record for the print edition is available from the British Library

Library of Congress Cataloging-in-Publication Data
A catalog record for the print edition is available from the Library of Congress

10 9 8 7 6 5 4 3 2 1
16 15 14 13 12

Illustrations by Toni Goffe

Design by Design Deluxe
Print edition typeset in 11pt Helevetica Neue LT Pro by 30
Print edition printed and bound in Great Britain by Henry Ling Ltd, at Dorset Press, Dorchester, Dorset

NOTE THAT ANY PAGE CROSS REFERENCES REFER TO THE PRINT EDITION

To Regina Clayton

An inspiration in taking on something important and saying YES.

Contents

About the author ix
Author's acknowledgements xi
Introduction xii

PART ONE Stuck on Yes 1

1 Meet the Gopher 3
2 Bury the Gopher 15

PART TWO YES or NO? 33

3 The meaning of NO 35
4 When to say 'YES' and when to say 'NO' 59
5 How to say 'YES' 91

PART THREE Choosing NO 105

6 The psychology of NO 107
7 Say 'NO' for now 125
8 The Yes/No Compass 139
9 How to say 'NO' 151

CLOSING THOUGHTS Super-NO 173

APPENDIX Saying 'NO' to ... 177

Colleagues and customers 177
Deals and decisions 178
Friends and family 179
Treats and temptations 180
Irrational thinking 181

WHO ELSE NEEDS *THE YES/NO BOOK*? 183

Also by Mike Clayton 185
Mike can say 'YES' to your organisation 186

About the author

Like many of his readers, Mike Clayton first became successful by saying 'yes' and delivering on his commitments. But as he experienced more and more calls on his time, he became aware that he was in danger of failing, and as he had more opportunities, he needed to find a way to choose which ones to follow.

Mike has been a successful project manager and management consultant, before changing career and becoming a successful coach and trainer, founding two training businesses. Now in his third career as a speaker and author, Mike has got more done than most, yet said NO to more things than he has said yes to.

Mike has been a Senior Manager at international consulting firm, Deloitte, a freelance trainer and coach, a company director, a school governor at two schools (serving as Chair of Governors at one) and a charity trustee. He is now in demand as a public speaker and is the author of eight books to date, including *Smart to Wise*, and four in Pearson Education's 'Brilliant' series.

The Yes/No Book is Mike's very personal take on how to get more done by knowing when to say 'YES', when to say 'NO', and how to do either with confidence and style.

Author's acknowledgements

The *Yes/No Book* began as two separate ideas: one when I developed my first time and workload management training programme in 2003, and another whilst on holiday with my wife (then, my wife to be), in 2007. Felicity has had to live with the Gopher since then! Indeed, she even had to humour my need, whilst in France, to look for, buy, and carry around a stuffed Gopher (*un gaufre en peluche*).

Thank you too, to Rachael Stock, my editor at Pearson, for helping me to shape this book, and to anyone who has attended one of my time management seminars – particularly those who took the trouble to ask me questions afterwards, and thereby helped me to clarify my thinking. I also want to thank the Alzheimer's Society for their support.

Finally, thank you, *gaufre en peluche*, for being the model for my Gopher sketches that helped indicate the drawings this book would need, and artist and friend, Toni Goffe for turning those sketches into artwork.

Introduction

Do you spend too much of your life doing what you think you ought to do rather than what you want to do?

Many of us do that. Indeed, many of us do not do what we think we ought to do: we do what we think the people around us think we ought to do.

It's time to focus a little more clearly on doing what *you* want. It's time to focus on doing the things that will bring you the life you want. It's time to make choices. It's time to know when to say 'YES' and when to say 'NO'.

But here's the problem. For most of us, the challenge is not to know what is right for us: it is to choose it. This challenge is about *how* to say 'YES' and *how* to say 'NO'.

If you have hopes, dreams, and a passion, you deserve the chance to fulfil them. It is the only way you have to make your life what you want rather than living the life that the people around you expect. So, you need to know what you want, and to become a little more resolute about getting it.

If this sounds selfish, then maybe it is and maybe that is no bad thing. Because, paradoxically, when you give more of your time to yourself and the things that matter most to you, you will have more time, energy and passion for giving generously to others.

The Yes/No Book

The Yes/No Book is about when to say 'yes' and when to say 'no'. It sounds so simple, yet too many of us are overwhelmed by obligations, because we find it hard to say 'yes' and 'no' at the right time and in the right way.

If you fear that you will limit your career or be disliked…

Or if you find you can't seem to make decisions and say the right thing at the right time…

Or if you find yourself ending up with more on your plate than you bargained for…

You need the power of YES and NO.

- **The Yes/No Book** shows you the problems that arise from an inability to say yes or no at the right times, and to the right things.
- **The Yes/No Book** shows you how to say 'no' properly. Not just saying 'no' but giving a positive answer; a Noble Objection. We make a Noble Objection when we decline to do something or accept an offer because there is a good reason for that objection.
- **The Yes/No Book** will help you decide when Yes or No is the right response.

- **The Yes/No Book** will show you when and how to say Yes or No and do it honestly and with confidence

- **The Yes/No Book** will give insights and practical techniques to take control of your decisions – and therefore of your life. It will give you more time to do what matters most and take you closer to the success and fulfilment you want.

Part one: Stuck on YES

Chapter 1: Meet the Gopher

Your inner Gopher is your tendency to 'go-for-this' and 'go-for-that' without discrimination. Consequently, you can find yourself tired, stressed and ineffective when it most matters. This introductory chapter looks at the Gopher's strengths and weaknesses, and the different types of Gopher.

Chapter 2: Bury the Gopher

How to leave your Gopher lifestyle behind and the benefits you can gain from being more proactive in choosing what to say 'yes' or 'no' to. We'll give Gophers four essential questions to ask, and four alternative strategies.

Part two: YES or NO?

Chapter 3: The meaning of NO

How can you say 'no' and stay popular? By transforming 'no' into 'N.O.' – a Noble Objection. You can use N.O. when you understand the distinction between 'Goal-directed choices' and 'Guilt-directed choices'. So, you will learn why it is vital to know what you want to achieve, and get the tools to figure it out.

Chapter 4: When to say 'YES' and when to say 'NO'

How to identify when to say 'NO' and when to say 'YES'. This chapter will give you the decision-making tools you need, and examine the criteria to apply, to assess what is the 'right' thing to do.

Chapter 5: How to say 'YES'

Saying 'yes' seems easy, but are you doing it on your own terms? Are you in control and do you know how to reap the real benefits of YES? This chapter looks at how to make the most of a decision to say 'YES', including ways to avoid purposeless procrastination.

Part three: Choosing NO

Chapter 6: The psychology of NO

Why do we find no so hard? We'll take a look at the psychology of no and how to overcome the hurdles of fear, guilt and discomfort.

Chapter 7: Say 'NO' for now

You will learn the distinction between 'time-critical' and 'time-charmed', and the value of purposive and purposeful procrastination: how deferring activities can get more done, when there is a 'right' time to do things, and the value of procrastination in creativity.

Chapter 8: The Yes/No Compass

Let's put goal-directed and time-charmed activities on the same page and create the Yes/No Compass: the ultimate tool to help you find your way through tricky time-management decisions. We'll also look at the OATS principle for planning your time.

Chapter 9: How to say 'NO'

This chapter will show you how to say 'NO' with confidence, good grace and authority, and how to leave people feeling positive about your NO. How can you spot and deal with manipulative behaviour, and counter attempts to change your mind? And when *should* you change your mind?

Off you go

Yes/No creates boundaries between will and won't, can and can't, want and don't want. Where are those boundaries, and who draws them? It is time for *you* to take charge of the two most important words in your vocabulary: YES and NO.

PART ONE

Stuck on Yes

CHAPTER 1

Meet the Gopher

How often do you have the feeling that you have spent your whole day being busy, but at the end of the day, you seem to have achieved very little? You should have a great sense of satisfaction from having done loads, but instead you have the empty feeling that little or none of it has been worthwhile.

Worse still, you also realise there are other things that you haven't achieved… and these are the ones you wish you'd had time to do. If you hadn't been so busy, then maybe you could have done something more useful instead.

You have become a victim of the Gopher.

The Gopher will see an opportunity or think of something that needs to be done, and it will always 'go for it'.

Where does the Gopher come from?

The Gopher is probably as old as humanity. It is wired into our unconscious and it is a response to fear. Our lives are full of opportunities to do things, requests for help, and jobs to be done. The natural thing to do when faced with this – your automatic reaction if you like – is to go for it. So, most of the time, you do… without even thinking.

But if you do pause for a moment and ask yourself '*What if I don't?*' then fear is often the answer. Fear that you will miss out, fear that you will disappoint someone, fear that you will suffer recriminations for not helping, fear that you will regret your decision in one way or another.

So, to protect you from all of this fear and angst, your unconscious will often just by-pass it and go straight to 'yes'. That unconscious drive to say 'yes' and to go for it is your Gopher.

And it is getting worse. As far back as 1970, Alvin Toffler coined the term '***overchoice***' to describe the surfeit of options we have. You would think that more choice is a good thing: more movies to see, more chocolate bars to try, more types of phone to buy. In fact, too many choices leave us fearful that we will make the wrong decision, leading us to less happiness, not more. This is what Barry Schwartz describes as '***the paradox of choice***' in his book of the same name (HarperCollins, 2004). The paradox of choice is that the more choices we have, the less happy we are. More choices make decision-making harder and satisfaction with your decision lower.

What is the Gopher?

The Gopher is your unconscious drive to say 'yes' and to go for it. It arises from three urges.

1 **Autopilot:** With lots of choices, there is too much demand on your conscious brain, so it settles into automatic responses. When you are asked for help or when you see a chance to do something, your first urge is to surrender your judgement to your autopilot and just go for it.

2 **Maximising:** You want the best, you want the most and you don't want to miss out. The only way to ensure you know what the best is, and that you don't miss out, is to try everything. The urge to maximise your opportunities is a strong one because it often leads to you getting the best – but rarely to being happy. Striving to maximise means you may get more than me, but you may never get enough for you. Is there more? Just in case, you had better go for it.

3 **Pleasing:** The need to please is embedded deeply in many of us, and this urge is more than willing to overcome your own happiness to do it. So, if I ask you for a favour, don't disappoint me: just go for it.

Are you a Gopher, a Beaver or a Dormouse?

While a Gopher will go for it and dissipate its energy across a lot of tasks, its friend the Beaver will beaver away, investing all of its energy in a single all-important task, until it is finished. Let's not forget the Dormouse. The Dormouse really can't be bothered; it would rather do something altogether less taxing instead.

Try our short quiz and see how much inner Gopher you have.

ARE YOU A GOPHER, A BEAVER OR A DORMOUSE?

1 The doorbell rings. It's your neighbour, asking if you can come round and give them a hand with something.

a You're busy and have a lot to get done today, but you offer to help out anyway.

b You are working on something important, so you apologise and ask if you can come round at the end of the day, when you'll be finished.

c You're not really doing very much, but you can't be bothered, so you say you are busy and apologise for not being able to help.

2 You look at your To Do list at the start of the morning and think about today…

a There's a lot to do and you are going to be busy fitting it all in, and then you think of a couple more things to add to the list.

b You scan your list, to focus on one or two things that are important, and then you think about when you are going to work on them.

c You don't like the look of that: best get a cup of coffee and check out your Facebook page or flick through the magazine on the shelf.

3 It's the weekend and there isn't anything in your diary and there isn't anything you need to do.

  a Not to worry, you'll find plenty of things to get on with – magazines to read, chores to do, jobs around the house, cleaning the car... Of course there are things you need to do.

  b What a marvellous opportunity to dedicate some time to a project or hobby that is important to you.

  c Aaahhh lovely! Someone put the kettle on for me.

4 At the end of a typical working day you look back.

  a You don't feel as if you have been particularly effective – but at least you got loads done and everyone who asked for something got a response. If only you could have done that thing you planned to do by lunchtime. Never mind: tomorrow.

  b You have made significant progress on the most important projects, and dealt effectively with the critical issues that cropped up.

  c Hmmm. Perhaps you could have done more, but you don't think anyone noticed.

5 Think about all of the projects you have on at the moment.

  a Wow! You have a lot of projects, all demanding your time. They all seem important, but how will you make progress with all of them?

    b That's just the right balance. A few well-chosen projects that you are fully committed to, and that will make a real difference.

    c Lots of ideas but nothing much to show for them. You really must make a proper start with one or two projects.

6 An article catches your attention and gives you a great idea for a new project.

    a Great, you'll get started on it straight away.

    b You decide to think it through carefully and maybe talk to a couple of people before deciding how important your idea is.

    c Maybe you are too busy at the moment. It doesn't seem that good an idea. If it is, someone else can pick it up.

How did you answer those questions?

Most answers were a

Well, at least you have the right book in your hands: you're a Gopher. Now, suppress your desire to skim this book and then move quickly on to something else. Read it carefully.

Most answers were b

Congratulations, you're a Beaver. This book wasn't written for you, but you saw it and decided that there is something in it for you, so you will probably make time to read it carefully and find the ideas that will make a difference.

Most answers were c

You don't have trouble saying 'no': you're a Dormouse. Your problem is saying 'yes'. Perhaps you should skip straight to Chapter 5. Do it now. I know you'd rather switch on the TV, but this matters.

The advantages and disadvantages of being a Gopher

We all have a bit of Gopher in us, and that's good. But too much Gopher behaviour can be a problem. Let's look at what's good and what's bad about being a Gopher.

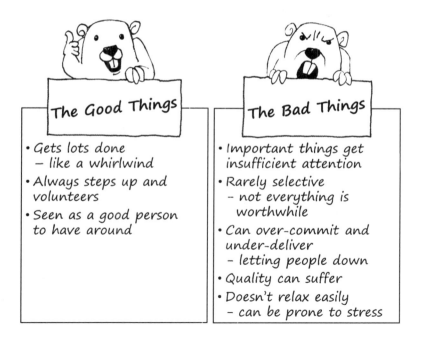

The Good Things

- Gets lots done
  – like a whirlwind
- Always steps up and volunteers
- Seen as a good person to have around

The Bad Things

- Important things get insufficient attention
- Rarely selective
  – not everything is worthwhile
- Can over-commit and under-deliver
  – letting people down
- Quality can suffer
- Doesn't relax easily
  – can be prone to stress

Gophers are generally productive and they seem to generate a lot of energy. But sometimes there is more heat than light: not only is their energy poorly focused, it isn't always effective.

The problem with the Gopher is its tendency to rush in without thinking, often creating its own problems. There is nothing wrong with going for it – it is a commendable trait. What is important is knowing what to go for, and when to go for it.

Meet the family

The Gopher is not alone. There is a whole family of Gophers that each has its own motivations for behaving as it does. Let's meet the family.

All of us can act in each of these ways at some time or other, but when you feel stressed or under pressure, one of them is likely to dominate. Which one you favour will probably depend on the choices and experiences you have had from your earliest days, as a child. This means that one of these Gophers may be more familiar to you than the others because it has been running your life from childhood.

Day-to-day, however, when you are not under particular pressure, you will experience each of these Gophers, as your attitudes to yourself (whether you feel good about yourself or not) and others (whether they seem OK to you or not) vary.

Eager Gopher

Eager Gophers feel good about themselves and they respect the people around them, so they are keen to get on with anything that they are asked to do. But they are Gophers, so they are rarely selective about what they take on. They feel as if it is only by going for it that they will retain the liking and trust of those other people.

Eager Gophers do not believe, deep down, that they are wholly OK. Rather, it feels that they will only be OK if they go for it. Eager Gophers go for it to make themselves feel OK, whether by pleasing the people around them, by meeting some internal standard of perfection, by showing how strong and capable they are, by continuing to try hard, or simply by hurrying up and getting on with it.

If, in the moment, you feel completely OK about yourself, you will have no trouble saying 'no', and letting your inner Beaver focus on what is really important.

Submissive Gopher

Submissive Gophers do not feel OK about themselves. Instead, they feel as if everyone else is stronger, more confident and more OK than they are. So they try to get away from that feeling by taking on tasks, which they hope will relieve the pressure that they feel to conform or to perform. They don't feel good about going for it; in fact, it can be exhausting. But at least they can get away from the constant demands on them.

Submissive Gophers often miss out on the important opportunities in life. They feel others are more important, more deserving and just better than they are, so they adopt a kind of victimised helplessness – often declaring '*Poor me – look at how much pressure you are putting me under.*'

Ironically, by conforming to this mental script and going for whatever other people want of them, Submissive Gophers are reinforcing the harmful belief that others are better than they are. Until you confront your Submissive Gopher with the simple fact that you are every bit as good as anyone else – and have as much right as they do to make choices about your life – your Submissive Gopher will continue to make your life a misery.

Despairing Gopher

For Despairing Gophers, life can seem futile. It feels as if no one will help them, so they do things out of desperation, with no real hope that they will make any difference. They might as well go for it; there is nothing else they can do.

And often, Despairing Gophers will want to freeze and do nothing. They will then feel guilty about not doing anything, but will blame circumstances or others for putting them in that position.

Despairing Gophers will go through the motions, but feel as if they are getting nowhere with what they are doing. Each time they go for it, it will be ultimately futile, because there will just be more demands on them later; yet none of them will make any difference.

Despairing Gophers feel put-upon and unloved. Their sense of the world is totally distorted. If a Despairing Gopher is in charge of your life, you need to take on the two big issues that it presents you with: to believe in yourself, and to believe in others. The actions you take can make a difference to you and your world, because you have an important part to play in it. And other people have an important part to play in your life: they can help you and bring you pleasure.

Arrogant Gopher

Arrogant Gophers seem to be always looking for ways to put others down. Taking on tasks is one more way to demonstrate their superiority. They do so angrily. They resent the intrusion, and only accede to the task to get rid of the other person and to reinforce their belief that they can't trust anybody else to do it properly and that the only solution is to do it yourself.

Arrogant Gophers are superficially in charge, but when you behave this way habitually, rather than on the odd occasion when you are highly stressed, you will start building up resentment from the people around you. Arrogant Gophers are neither liked nor respected by others.

Just as Submissive Gophers must learn to respect themselves, Arrogant Gophers must learn to respect other people and recognise that they are every bit as good, worthy and capable as they are.

Yes/No in an instant

The Gopher goes for this – goes for that. It gets loads done but rarely feels in control. There is a whole family of gophers eagerly, submissively, despairingly and arrogantly going for it without much thought for when it is right to say 'yes', and when it is right to say 'no'.

Yes/No: Do you have an inner Gopher?

Yes/No: Are you ready to bury it?

CHAPTER 2

Bury the Gopher

There is no doubt that Gophers are a nuisance. So you need to bury them and keep them out of your way, then you can focus on what is important and feel more in control. Let's look at the why and the how of Gopher-burying, and then find some practical questions to ask that will help you to know when and how to bury your inner Gopher.

Why bury the Gopher?

There are lots of good reasons to bury your inner Gopher. Let's take a look at some of them.

- Important things get done
- More satisfaction from the things you do
- Time to meet your commitments...
  ... and do them well
- People have new respect for you
- More control over your workload
- More time to relax and enjoy life

Important things get done

The first thing you gain when you bury your Gopher is the time you need to do the things that matter. You will start to notice that the important things get done and, as a result, you will feel like you are starting to make progress with your goals, your projects, your career, and your life.

More satisfaction from the things you do

When you have the time to beaver away at the important things, two things will happen. The first is that you will get a lot of satisfaction from completing them. This is not just the knowledge that something important is done – which is a great satisfaction – but also the knowledge that you have done it well and given it the time and attention it deserves.

The second is that you will get satisfaction from doing the things you do because you have chosen to do them. When your mind is not distracted by Gopher-level activities, you can focus on what really matters and be able to enjoy doing it – whatever it is.

Time to meet your commitments...
... and do them well

When you bury your Gopher, you will only take on commitments to other people that you choose to take on. And, because there will be fewer of them, you will have more time for them, and feel less pressured by them. They will seem less of a chore and, because you have more time for them, you will find that the quality of your work on them will improve.

People have new respect for you

The increasing quality of your work is one reason why people will have a new respect for you. But by far the greater reason is that you are no longer a yes-woman or yes-man, saying 'yes' to everything and therefore truly committing to nothing. Now, rather than being the doormat, you are the door, blocking the way to requests that do not suit you.

When you say 'yes' now, you are saying 'yes' for a good reason. Your choices are strategic: you are thinking about what is important for you, for your team, and for the organisation you work for. And you are investing your time wisely, which will deliver a good return.

More control over your workload

Having fewer things to do, having the time to focus on what's important, and feeling able to say 'no' to meaningless tasks, will give you more control of how you use your time. You can now schedule when to tackle your jobs with more confidence, and start to feel in control of your workload. You can start to balance how much you set out to achieve with the time you choose to make available. In that time you can beaver away at making a difference, and get more done.

More time to relax and enjoy life

Feeling that you aren't in control leads to stress. Your inner Gopher is a stress-making behaviour pattern. When you bury it, stress will start to fall away, because you – not it – are in control.

The added benefit is that you will now have more time to relax and enjoy your life. Your life will become what *you* choose it to be; not what others specify and you accede to, through the actions of your inner Gopher.

How to bury the Gopher

This section is not yet about how to say 'no'. You'll need to be a little patient and wait for the next chapter, Chapter 3, to start learning that important skill.

First, before you can say 'no' confidently, you have to learn how to bury your inner Gopher: how to conquer your urges to go for this and go for that, without thinking. This section is about changing the way you think, fundamentally, about your time. There are three steps to take, and some exercises that will help you along the way.

Step 1: Focus on the things you can control or influence

The control paradox

There are some things in life that you can control – and others that you can't. Spending your time going for this and going for that, in an attempt to control the things you cannot control is futile. Yet we often do, without thinking.

The paradox is that the more we focus on the things we want to control, the more aware we become that we are failing, and the greater the need we feel to control them. There is no end to this cycle of increasingly more futile attempts to wrestle control.

What you have to do is break the cycle. You can do this by changing your focus on to the things that you can control. When you do this, your actions have a real effect on the world – your job, your family or your aspirations. This will give you a sense of achievement and well-being that leads to a far more positive cycle.

Step 2: Consciously slow yourself down

Slow down

There is a proverb: *'more haste: less speed'*. When you get yourself into a busy-busy, got-to-go-for-it mindset, it is hard to be effective in what you do. This leads to mistakes and wasted effort that actually hold you back.

When you slow down deliberately, your responses and your work are more considered and careful. This means that you can get more done, to a higher standard. So make a conscious effort to be deliberate and to take the important things more slowly.

Step 3: Have the flexibility to say 'yes' to exciting opportunities

Embrace serendipity

Serendipity (n): *'an unexpected discovery, made by chance'.*

Focus and a determination that you can say 'no' when it is the right thing to say, are important, but never let your focus become tunnel vision. If you do, you will miss the wider world of beauty and the opportunities that surround you.

When you know not just what you are focusing on but also why it is important, then you will be able to spot the opportunities that will give you more of what you want, more easily.

Burying the Gopher will give you more space in your life to seize opportunities and embrace the joys of the moment. Make a conscious effort to look around you and see what is out there, just waiting for you to take advantage of it.

Exercises to help you bury the Gopher

Burying your inner Gopher means becoming expert at taking time for yourself and what is important to you. Here are six ways you can start to hone that skill.

Evaluation

Most of us have a To Do list somewhere – in our notebooks, on a scrap of paper, electronically, or just in our heads. Examine it critically.

First, look for the longest-range project that you have on your list. If there is nothing that contributes to a project that lasts as long as a year, then that should tell you something! But let's say you have a couple of tasks that are part of a project that will only be complete in two years. Two years now becomes your time frame.

Now look at the list and mentally or physically cross off all of the things that really do not matter. These are things that you know you ought to say 'no' to; that you ought not to take on. To help you, you may want to consider their importance in the scale of your time frame. In our example, how important will they seem two years from now?

Finally, shift your perspective. If your time frame is two years, ask yourself, *'What if I only had two years to live?'* Would this be a 'yes' task or a 'no' task?

Savouring your experiences

Pick one experience each day and experience it one hundred per cent. Savour every last moment of it. One day it may be your lunch; another, a conversation with a friend or colleague. It may be a work task, or a chore at home, like washing up, gardening or mending a tap. It may be something as simple as drinking a cup of tea. Take the time to notice all of the details. Do it steadily, with no rush to complete it. Savour it for what it is. When you start to experience every last gram of experience, the tasks you choose to take on will seem more fulfilling, and meaningless tasks will start to seem more of a waste of your valuable time.

Thinking time

Once a week, give yourself at least half an hour of high-quality head-space. Take time to think about anything and nothing. Find a park bench, a comfy sofa, or a pleasant café that is not intrusively noisy. Pick a time when it is not frequented by friends and colleagues. Go there alone and take nothing except a pen and paper. Get yourself a drink and spend your time thinking.

If something is on your mind, turn it over and see what's underneath. If you are working on a project or initiative at home or at work, think through what might be coming up. If there's nothing much on your mind, let it wander. Often, this is the most valuable time of your week, so don't waste it by being a Gopher and trying to do something.

A useful tip is to set yourself a question before you take yourself off for your thinking time. Perhaps, *'What am I missing?'* or *'What next?'* Maybe *'How can I do this?'* or *'What can I learn from that?'*

Giving time

How about giving somebody some of your time? What could be better training to repress the over-eager Gopher than to stop and give? Think of someone important in your life – a colleague, a friend, a family member – and set a time with them that you can spend together. Then give them your absolute and complete attention. Listen to them, respond to their agenda, do what they want to do. It is their time, not yours.

Go for a walk

Nothing recharges your batteries and relieves stress as simply, easily and time/effort-effectively as getting up and going for a walk. Energy flows, blood flows, your parasympathetic nervous system is revived, your breathing and posture improve, and your mind starts to access the unconscious thoughts that have been going on over the last hours or even days.

Movement is a therapy, but it also exercises your Gopher's need to get up and go for it, without going for something you should be saying 'no' to.

Holidays and breaks

A classic Gopher problem is an inability to allow itself a proper break – or, when compelled to take a break, to properly enjoy it. So consult your loved ones and book a holiday. Don't put it off with the expectation that you will grab a last-minute holiday. Sit down and plan a real break that you will enjoy. Clear your diary – ideally taking an extra day off work on the day before your break starts – and book something good.

Four questions for Gophers

One of the dangers that faces a Gopher mentality is the never-ending To Do list. No matter how well you do, your inner Gopher will find more things to keep adding to the list and, therefore, more things to go for.

You may not be able to bury the Gopher straight away, but let's start by putting it in its place. This means addressing the To Do list that keeps on growing. You can do this by asking four crucial questions whenever you feel your inner Gopher is pulling you to go for it.

Question 1: *'What if I don't do it?'*

This question is about consequences. What can you realistically expect to happen if you do not go for it? To what extent are the consequences acceptable to you?

Get into the habit of asking this question, and you may be surprised about how often the answer is *'nothing'* or, at least, *'nothing much'*. Often this will apply to the tasks you have at the bottom of your To Do list: the ones that get copied from one To Do list to the next, when you've completed all but the last few things. You feel like you should go for them – in fact you feel guilty that you haven't. But you've been putting them off for days, weeks, or even months.

So, if you do find the answer is *'nothing'* or *'nothing much'*, then cross those things off your list and savour the sense of release you get from having decided that you won't go for it after all.

If you have trouble with this, try taking it off your To Do list, and transferring it to a new list, on a new sheet of paper – a To Don't list. Keep it somewhere safe, but out of the way.

Example

Martin and Jean moved to a new house and immediately made a list of small improvements and jobs to do. One month later, all but five were done. Six months later, Martin still looked at the list every weekend but found excuses not to tackle any of the jobs. There were still five things on the list. Finally, he realised that throwing the list away was not going to make him any less likely to do the jobs, but it would stop him fretting about them every weekend.

Notice that you may find cases when you ask *'What if I don't do it?'* and you get an answer like: *'I'd be fine with it – my boss will be furious.'* What does this mean?

It means that you may not be looking far enough ahead. Perhaps what you should have thought was: *'My boss will be furious – it could affect my appraisal – my career could be harmed.'* If you are fine with that, then don't do it, but burying your inner Gopher must not compromise your long-term priorities. If you realise that this isn't the career for you, it's time to stop going for this career. Otherwise, burying your inner Gopher is not a sound excuse for not doing the jobs at work that you don't like.

Let's assume you must do it. What next?

Question 2: *'What if I only do part of it?'*

Once again, look at the consequences of splitting the task up, or of doing it to a different standard from the one you might carelessly assume is needed. Can you make the task smaller, to free up time for other things?

Assess the completion criteria objectively. Think about the people who will evaluate what you do and ask yourself – and them: *'What does "done" need to look like?'* We often set or expect standards without careful thought.

Sometimes *'good enough'* is not what you want: you want *'the best possible'*. But in most circumstances, anything better than good enough is a waste of effort that will diminish your capacity to do everything you need. Understand what you are doing it for, and limit your ambition to go for the best to the times when the best will make a difference. All other times, deliver *'done'* to meet the needs of the situation.

Example

Victoria had to produce a management report every month. It was a 20-page document with lots of detailed analysis. One month she was extremely busy with a critical project and found herself short of time. She simplified the report and presented five pages of graphs and tables, each with a headline describing the key things that it illustrated. It took her a fraction of the time. When they received it, all of the directors were highly complimentary about the new format she had developed and urged her to keep that format.

You won't always be able to diminish the task at hand, so what next?

Question 3: *'What if I do it later?'*

Don't just go for it without assessing when it is needed and when would be the best time for you to attend to it. *'Right, I'll do it straight away'* sounds positive and enthusiastic, and can get you into all sorts of time-management troubles. How about: *'Right, leave it with me, I'll do it in good time for the deadline.'*

When you understand time priorities and can schedule tasks to suit you, you gain control and give things the time they need, without feeling rushed. They don't interfere with what you are doing now, so your work also becomes more efficient and effective.

Another source of pressure from your inner Gopher to go for it are all those aspirational tasks and projects on your To Do list. You want to get started on all of them, but you've been putting them off because you don't feel like you have enough time. This can cause stress – a tension between wanting to go for it and knowing the time is not right.

The solution is to take those things off your To Do list. They don't belong on your To Don't list, so you need a new list: a Will Do list. Your Will Do list is the first step in planning how and when you will do something. It contains a clear description of what you plan to do and two essential dates: a start date – when you will start work on getting it done; and a finish date – when you propose to have it completed.

What this does is turn a pesky To Do item into the start of a plan. By defining a start and end date, you have turned it into a project – maybe it is just a mini-project, but it gives you a recognition that this needs thought and sets a time to do it. Now it isn't a To Do item prodding away at your inner Gopher, it's a plan. Now you have taken control and you will find a great deal less stress associated with it.

Example

Gregor was a highly productive salesperson and kept a full To Do list. But there were three big items on it that seemed to get bumped from one To Do list to the next. These were great ideas, but his busy schedule did not permit him to tackle them. Whenever he put them on to a new To Do list, he felt miserable. But he certainly didn't want to abandon these great initiatives to a To Don't list. So he started a new page in his notebook for the first one, wrote it at the top and, on the next line, wrote '*Plan for completion by the end of November*'. For the second, he blocked out some time in his diary in two days' time, to get started. And for the third, he replaced the words '*new sales initiative*' with '*Speak to Carolyn about a possible new sales initiative*'. Now he felt he had made some progress on all three.

You may not be able to reschedule it until later. What next?

Question 4: *'What if someone else does it?'*

Does it have to be you? Is there really nobody else who could do it? Part of the mentality of many Gophers is the belief that:

- *'I'm the only one who can do this'* or
- *'Others could do it – but not as well'.*

Some even fear:

- *'If I don't do it, someone else will get the credit'.*

Well, you are rarely the only person who could do a good job, even if others would do it differently. Sometimes, they will do it better, but even if they don't, if they never get a chance to learn, then you'll be stuck in an endless cycle. So, you worry about the credit. Don't. If you can identify the right person for the job in a few minutes, then that is a capability people will value.

Sometimes, the answer to this question is delegation: giving your task to someone else to do for you. Sometimes it is about abdication: recognising that it is not important enough to you for you to do it and leaving it for someone else to pick up, if it is important enough to them.

Sometimes, however, you will realise you do need to do it; you need to do all of it; you need to do it now; and only you can do it. Now your inner Gopher has lost control. You are going to do it, not because the Gopher made you, but because *you* decided that it is the right thing to do.

Top tip

Make yourself small cards – or download one from www.theyesnobook.co.uk – with the four questions for Gophers on them. Put the cards in your pockets and your bags, so you always have one ready to hand, wherever you are.

What if ...
   I **don't** do it?

What if ...
   I only do **part** of it?

What if ...
   I do it **later?**

What if ...
   someone else does it?

A new kind of Gopher

These four questions may not be enough to bury your inner Gopher forever, but they will at least enable you to swap it for a new one. In the next chapter you will start to learn how to say 'no', but for now, you have four questions that will allow you to unleash your Selective Gopher. The Selective Gopher is you, in charge of making careful decisions about what you go for and what you don't.

Selective Gopher:
- considers consequences
- makes choices
- goes for it sometimes
- says no sometimes
- delivers consistently
- earns respect
- is under **your** control

Yes/No in an instant

There are many good reasons to bury your inner Gopher. To do so, you need to get comfortable with saying no. Start to focus on the things you can control, slow yourself down, and stay flexible so that you can embrace new opportunities. When you feel tempted to go for it, ask yourself the four questions.

Yes/No: Have you found a change you can make, to start to bury your inner Gopher?

Yes/No: Do you have the four questions for Gophers ready to hand?

Yes/No: Are you ready to start saying 'no'?

PART TWO

YES or NO?

CHAPTER 3

The meaning of NO

*'The art of leadership is saying no, not yes.
It is very easy to say yes'*

Tony Blair

Stuck?

Many people are.

If you feel trapped by your life, your job, or your circumstances, it may not be because you said 'yes' to the wrong things. You may well be saying yes to precisely the *right* things.

The problem is that you may not have the time or the energy to devote to them, because you are *also* saying 'yes' to a load of other stuff: stuff you ought to say 'no' to. Only when you have the courage to say 'no' to them will you be able to commit enough time to the things you want to focus on; the things you ought to focus on.

Only when you have the courage to say 'no' will wholly new possibilities emerge.

The power of 'no'

'No' is an enormously powerful word, but it takes practice to get used to using it with confidence. There was a stage in your life, however, when you used it a lot. When you were a toddler, you liked to say 'no'. All toddlers do: it's a stage. They even seem to say 'no' to the things they like. Why is that?

'No' gives you control and what toddlers start to do is to exert control over their environment and the people in it: their carers and families. This means a constant stream of 'no, no, no!' Yes and no, used properly, are our ultimate control mechanisms in a social world. Toddlers are learning their power. As adults, we often forget this lesson. Childhood experiences taught your inner Gopher that it's not OK to say 'no'.

Noble objection

'No' is a difficult word for most adults to use, and the principal reason is because it sounds negative to us.

No: *'negative answer to a question; used to express denial, refusal, disagreement.'*

And who wants to appear to be negative? Most of us don't really want to be negative, so even seeming to be negative to your colleagues, friends and family is a mortifying prospect. So, perhaps it's better if you just grit your teeth, and say 'yes'.

Saying 'yes'

Saying 'yes' is a strategy that may have served you well in the past. You started your career by being good at saying 'yes', by delivering on your promises, and by building a reputation for being someone people could go to, to get things done. 'Yes' worked for you: it was a good ally.

> *'Conscientious people will always take responsibility for the commitments that they make.'*

The problem is this: as you move through your career and your life, there are more and more things to say 'yes' to. Eventually you start to reach a point where you simply cannot manage all of them. To avoid disappointing others, you start to fail on the commitments you make to yourself: your priorities start to slip.

> *'Self-control means only making commitments that you are able to honour.'*

If you believe that your future success is linked to saying 'yes' to everything, you're in trouble. Early in your career, it may be that people respected you for being good at 'yes'. But at some stage, this will not be enough to earn you respect. Instead, it will do little more than make you a doormat: someone people go to because they know you will say 'yes', without thinking.

You may fear that saying 'no' will alienate them. So you continue to say 'yes' to keep their friendship and respect. It won't work. You may keep their friendship, but you will not maintain their respect.

Only when you learn to say 'no' properly can you regain people's respect. And if you do it properly, you can maintain and enhance their friendship too. Now you will not be a doormat: instead, you will become a careful thinker who commits to the important requests and has the time to honour those commitments and deliver on them to the highest standard. You are also someone for whom life is not cluttered by busy-busy, rush-rush meaningless activities. You have become someone of substance.

Turning 'no' into a positive

We've seen that the negative connotations of 'no' are a barrier to feeling confident about using the word. So I want to introduce you to a radical concept: the idea that 'no' can be a positive word.

1 Start by acknowledging the power of 'no', by giving it capital letters: NO.
2 Now notice that NO is not a word, it is an acronym: N.O.
3 N.O. stands for Noble Objection: what could be more positive than something that is 'noble'?

N.O. (acronym): 'Noble Objection: declining to do something for good reasons; making a positive choice to say "no", and doing so respectfully.'

A '*Noble Objection*' is when you choose to say 'NO' (for ease of use, we shall omit the full stops from here on) for reasons that you can wholly defend. It lies at the core of *The Yes/No Book*. Notice that it does not give you licence to say 'no' to your boss because you don't like the task they give you, or to say 'no' to your partner, because you can't be bothered. Neither of those is noble.

Rather, a Noble Objection is characterised by nobility: making ethical choices, and doing so with dignity. Therefore the two aspects of a Noble Objection are the following:

1 What you say 'NO' to: Choosing to make a Noble Objection for the right reasons, being mindful of consequences to you, to others, and to your relationships with them.

2 How you say 'NO': Making your Noble Objection in a way that lets people know that your choice is well made and leaving them feeling comfortable about your decision.

When you combine these two aspects of a Noble Objection, it becomes possible to say 'NO' with complete integrity.

Looking for 'NO's

'Yes' can steal your time. So, to start to understand how and when you give up your valuable time by using 'yes', think back over the last week. What things could you have 'NO'd? When could you have made a Noble Objection and freed up time for something more valuable? Here is a short exercise.

---

1 Take a sheet of paper and list the things you did last week, which you could have 'NO'd instead. To help you, think about these questions.

- What things did you do last week that had no value for you or the person who asked you to do it?

- What things did you do last week that could equally well have been done by somebody else? (Perhaps even done better?)

- What things did you do last week that you knew you shouldn't have taken on the moment you said 'yes'?

- What things did you do last week that made you feel angry, bitter or resentful of the imposition?

- What things did you do last week that turned out to be a complete waste of your time?

- What things did you do last week that caused you more stress, anxiety or hassle than they were worth?

- What things did you do last week that were just to please someone, to stop them from hassling you, or because you feared they wouldn't like you if you said 'no'?

- What things did you do last week that stopped you doing something more important?

2 How many things are there?

3 Now, against each item, make a note of the approximate time you spent on each thing. Add all this up. How much time did you spend on things you could have 'NO'd? How much time could you have freed up for other things?

4 Was this a typical week?

5 Now, against each of the things you said 'yes' to, put the name of the person to whom you said 'yes'. Do one or two names appear time after time? Is this typical?

- What does this tell you about your relationship with that person?

- How valuable is that relationship to you?

- Is saying 'yes' as often as you do consistent with achieving the relationship you want with that person? (It may be.)

You can find a worksheet for this exercise at www.theyesnobook.co.uk

---

One simple way to help remind yourself is to make a little 'tent card' to put on your desk or workbench, or by your phone. You can download a template from www.theyesnobook.co.uk

YES and NO

Knowing when to use your 'NO', and when to say a whole-hearted 'YES' is critical. We will look at this in great detail in Chapter 4, but here, we need to understand the underlying principle. It is time to learn about the distinction between *'Goal-directed activities'* and *'Guilt-directed activities'*.

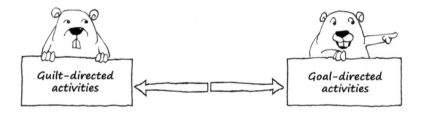

Goal-directed activities

Goal-directed activities are the things that you must do, you want to do, make a real difference to what you can achieve in your life, in your work, in your vocation. They are things you do because they are right and because you believe in them.

Goal-directed activities are driven by your passion and they take you towards the future you are committed to. You are drawn towards your goal-directed activities by aspiration, hope and idealism, and you do them for yourself and for the people you love.

These are the activities to say YES to. Not just a feeble 'yes', but a wholehearted, all-body YES signifying true commitment – because these are the activities that will contribute to your sense of fulfilment, success and happiness.

Guilt-directed activities

Guilt-directed activities are the things that you ought to do, you should do, and you feel guilty if you don't do. They are the things that *'they say you ought to do'* and you do them purely to please other people. Your motivations are usually duty or loyalty to people and institutions that no longer serve you well and you are driven to do them often out of fear of the consequences of not doing them.

Alternatively, guilt-directed activities are ones you do because of a guilty conscience, in atonement for some imagined or real transgression. Sometimes you do them to escape from a deeper, more important responsibility.

Guilt-directed activities are the ones to say 'NO' to. Make a Noble Objection to doing things out of fear, to escape responsibilities, or to assuage your guilt. These activities will bring you stress and disillusionment, and will ultimately block any sense of fulfilment and frustrate the level of material success you can achieve.

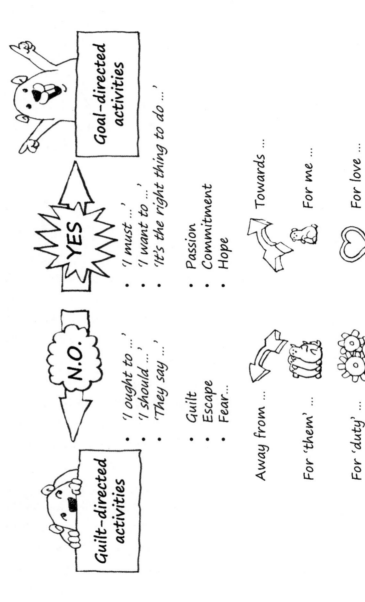

Goal-directed activities

YES

- 'I must ...'
- 'I want to ...'
- 'It's the right thing to do ...'

- Passion
- Commitment
- Hope

Towards ...

For me ...

For love ...

N.O.

- 'I ought to ...'
- 'I should ...'
- 'They say ...'

- Guilt
- Escape
- Fear...

Guilt-directed activities

Away from ...

For 'them' ...

For 'duty' ...

Desire-directed activities

Focusing on goal-directed activities will bring you what psychologists call '*eudaimonic happiness*'. This is the happiness, contentment and well-being we feel when we are happy with our lives. You are doing things that are true to yourself. You feel a sense of:

- **autonomy:** you get to make the choices about your life and how you live it
- **competence:** you get to do the things you are good at and enjoy
- **relatedness:** you get to have secure and fulfilling relationships with the people you choose
- **meaning:** you feel a sense of purpose and value in the things that you do
- **growth:** you feel that the choices you make are leading you to develop in positive ways.

But psychologists have identified another kind of happiness, which they call '*hedonic happiness*'. This is all about pleasure and joy in the moment. This is different from the happiness you will achieve through a focus on goal-directed activities, but I certainly wouldn't want you to associate joy and pleasure with guilt. Hedonic activities are neither guilt- nor goal-directed pleasures. They take you in a new direction: the direction of pure desire.

Desire-directed activities are the things that you do to enjoy the moment. They are an immersion in the now, rather than being focused on the past (as guilt-directed activities are) or the future (as goal-directed activities are). You do them not because you must, nor because you should: you do them because you want to. You do them for yourself and you do them for love, and this makes desire-directed activities positive in the same way as goal-directed activities are.

A balanced and happy life is one where you are able to get the right mixture of goal- and desire-directed activities. You don't use constant hedonism as an escape from reality, but you don't abandon all opportunities to enjoy yourself, in favour of some longed-for future.

> *'All work and no play make Jack or Jane miserable, dull and unfulfilled.'*

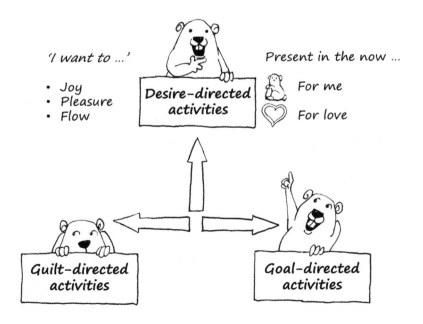

Displacement-directed activities

A final class of activities is those that you want to avoid: you are reluctant to do them despite knowing how important they are, and that they are, essentially, goal-directed. These tend to be things that seem difficult or unpleasant, so you put them off. You do something else instead: a '***displacement activity***'. This is an activity that displaces the other activity which would be a better use of your time.

You know you should say 'YES' but you'd rather do something more fun. So you put it off... for no better reason than '*I don't want to do it*' or '*I can't be bothered*'. This is '***purposeless procrastination***', and we'll tackle that head-on, in Chapter 5.

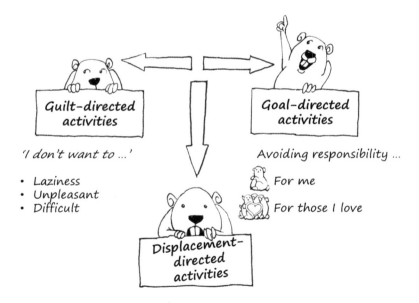

Know your goals

Focusing on goal-directed activities is all very well, but it does presuppose one thing: that you know what your goals are.

Let's start by defining '**goals**'. For our purposes, goals are what you want: they are the outcomes that will give you pride, satisfaction, pleasure…

We don't need to define them any more clearly than that, because sometimes they will be a small thing that can be achieved quickly and easily; at other times, they may be a whole change in every aspect of your life – or of the lives of others – that could take you a lifetime to achieve. You can set material goals, spiritual goals, intellectual or creative goals. You might share the task of achieving them with others, or the responsibility may be yours alone. They may be an end in themselves, or a step along the way. All that matters is you truly want to achieve the goal.

What do you want?

The challenge, of course, is to know what you want, so that you know what to say 'YES' or 'NO' to. Start by taking a notebook or a blank sheet of paper and write down whatever comes to mind, under the heading '*I want…*'.

For some people this will be enough or will give you a very clear idea of your goals. That's because many of us already have a pretty clear idea of what we want, and this is simply an opportunity to write it down.

THE EIGHT-PAGE METHOD

You can make the process more sophisticated by taking eight sheets of paper or eight pages in your notebook, and head them:

1 What I want in twenty years' time

2 What I want in ten years' time

3 What I want in five years' time

4 What I want in two years' time

5 What I want in one year's time

6 What I want in six months' time

7 What I want in three months' time

8 What I want in one month's time

Start with page one and put down everything you can think of. It is a long time horizon, so be ambitious for yourself.

> *'It's better to shoot for the stars and miss than to shoot for nothing and hit it.'*

Then go on to page two, then three and so on, until you reach your three-month goals. You may find that you want to repeat the same goal with a shorter time scale. That's fine; don't worry. When you have finished, go back over everything you have written and tidy it up.

You can find a worksheet for this exercise at www.theyesnobook.co.uk.

If you are not yet satisfied with your results, then you may need a more formal process, like the four-step process, below.

Four-step process for goal setting

This process for goal setting can take anything from 24 hours to a month, and most of this time will be spent in Step 1.

Step 1: Fermenting your goals

If you haven't thought very much about your goals before, then getting to an answer is not an instant process. You need to let your thoughts ferment, until they start to form clear ideas about what you want.

There are different ways to do this. You could combine various of these techniques.

- Relax, take your time, daydream and ponder.
- Take some long walks and clear your head, allowing thoughts to come.
- Ask yourself 'What do I want?' in the evening before you go to bed.
- Write:

> **MY GOALS**
> *Will I ...*

at the top of a sheet of paper and leave it on your table before you go to bed. Set your alarm early, get up the next morning and spend half an hour at the table, writing everything that comes into your head. Do this every day for a week.

- Chat about your goals and what you want with a trusted friend or partner.
- Think about all of the things that really excite and inspire you.
- Start a notebook and keep it with you. Write down ideas and goals whenever they come to you. And also write about those ideas and goals: for example, how you feel about them, what consequences they might have, and how you can make them real.
- Use the eight-page method.

Whichever of these techniques you use or combine; continue revisiting your goals from time to time, until you feel that you have some real understanding of what you want. Now it is time to write them down.

LOOKING FOR GREAT GOALS: KILLER QUESTIONS

One of the most powerful resources to help you find your goals is a question. Questions open up your thinking and the more spontaneous, unusual, disturbing they are, the more they will open your mind to new possibilities and help you to release suppressed dreams into your conscious awareness.

Some questions can have that kind of impact, from time to time. I call them '**killer questions**', and here are some of my favourites.

? What would you aim for if you had nothing to lose?

? If you learned you had only one year to live, what would you do?

? What do you really fear?

? Where did you dream you would be now when you were 16?

? Who do you look at with profound envy and think '*I could be what they are?*'

? What's the biggest lie you have been telling yourself and others?

? If you knew you would not fail, what would you aim for?

? What *else* is there, beyond your current priorities?

? When you daydream and fantasise, what truth is buried there?

? If all jobs paid the same, what would you do?

? What gives you a sense of invincible energy?

? When did you last feel really happy?

? What do you most fear to hear from someone you love?

? What question would you least like to be asked?

Step 2: Upsizing your goals

Take a look at each goal that you have written down. For each one, if you can, put a measure against it. What would be a good figure to aim for? You might have a salary goal, expressed in pounds per year. Or maybe you have a lifestyle goal and you want to be able to take five weeks of foreign holidays per year. Perhaps your goal is a beautiful home – on a scale of 1 (a hovel) to 100 (a palace), where does it sit? Maybe at 60?

When you have done that, review each figure and put a second figure next to it. What would be an outrageously impressive level to aim for? Double the salary, 12 weeks' holiday, a level 80 home. These are possible, but only with the greatest level of effort and performance from you.

So put a third figure, somewhere between the other two. Which would be a great goal to set yourself? That's the one to go for.

Write your goals out in full now, and write each one as an IOU.

> *IOU Inspirational – Outrageous*
> *– Uncomfortable*

- **Inspirational**: Make sure that each goal really grabs you by the gut and makes you want it like crazy.
- **Outrageous**: Set your goals to an outrageous level that will give you enormous satisfaction when you achieve them.
- **Uncomfortable**: Choose goals that will take you out of your comfort zone when you tackle the things that you will have to do to achieve them. If they are easy to achieve, how inspiring will they be?

Step 3: Writing yourself an IOU

The only thing you owe yourself in life is to live the best possible life that you can – to live the life you choose. Now write yourself that IOU. Summarise each IOU goal and write them all on one or more blank postcards. Carry these with you wherever you go. This IOU card will constantly inspire you by reminding you what to say 'YES' to, and when to say 'NO'.

You can find a template for your IOU cards at www.theyesnobook.co.uk

---

Will I? How to write your IOU

Recent research* shows a surprising result. Among subjects asked to express their goals in writing, those who wrote them in the conventional way: '*I will...*' performed less well than those who wrote them in the form: '*Will I...?*'

It seems that framing your goals as a question activates your brain more effectively. At the moment, the research has only examined short-term goal performance, but my current recommendation is that you write each of your goals in your IOU as a question or ponder:

'Will I... ?'

* Senay, I. Albarracín, D. and Noguchi, K. (2010) 'Motivating goal-directed behavior through introspective self-talk', *Psychological Science*, 21 (4): 499–50.

Step 4: Successorising your goals

It's now time to surround each goal with the accessories that it needs to make it realistic and achievable.

1 For each goal, write down what it will mean to you to achieve it. What is really inspiring about that goal?

2 Now write down how you will know for sure that your goal has been met. Give yourself an explicit completion criterion for each goal: '*When I have achieved my goal I will know it, because...* '.

3 Put together a plan.

- What are the steps along the way?
- What skills and knowledge do you need to acquire?
- Who are the people who can help you?
- What resources (things, equipment, money) do you need?
- What milestones are there along the way?

4 Finally, make your goals public. Tell people about them. Don't just pick one person and tell them everything, tell different people different goals. The more you share your goals with other people, the stronger you will find your commitment is to those goals. If you don't feel it appropriate to share a goal, then write it down and put it in an envelope addressed to yourself, with the completion date on the envelope. Post it.

When it arrives, put it safely in a drawer, ready for you to open on the date on the envelope.

Open on
31 December 2022

1st Class

A. Gopher
The Gopher Mound
Gauffreville
Hampe-agiter

Goals in your daily life

One of the most valuable aspects of goal setting is its ability to motivate and energise you to do even the most mundane – but necessary – tasks. When you set your goals for each week or each day, then make sure that you check to see how each one supports and reinforces your bigger goals. When you do that, you will see a new meaning and purpose in what you are doing at the daily level – even if it does not, superficially, appear to be delivering you your goals.

Yes/No in an instant

Stop seeing 'no' as a negative. No can be positive when you say it for the right reasons and you say it well: it becomes noble – a Noble Objection. Say 'YES' to goal-directed activities and 'NO' to guilt-directed activities. Allow yourself time for the pleasures of desire-directed activities and reject the futility of displacement-directed activities.

Yes/No: Are you committed to making a Noble Objection to things that will truly waste your time?

Yes/No: Are you ready to think carefully about when to say 'YES' and when to say 'NO'?

CHAPTER 4

When to say 'YES' and when to say 'NO'

'Yes and no, used properly, are our ultimate control mechanisms in a social world.'

There is an unfortunate paradox at the heart of how human beings use the words yes and no.

If I ask you to do something for me, then if I get anything other than a wholehearted 'yes', I had better treat it as a 'no'. If I don't, then I am setting myself up for disappointment. Somewhere along the line, you may forget my request, or put it to the back of the queue. Before I know it, any deadlines will be fast approaching, and you will be nowhere to be found. I'll get stressed and, when I remind you of your promise, so will you. Unless, of course, we get into an argument about whether or not you ever made a promise in the first place.

I am sure that sounds familiar, so let's look at the other side of the paradox. I ask you to do something for me and you'd rather not. But not wanting to upset me, you say something equivocal. You are careful not to say 'yes', but you cleverly manage to avoid saying 'no'. Now, despite wanting to feel free of the task, with a clear conscience, you cannot help but feel a little responsible. Not saying 'yes' is not the same as saying 'no' and now your inner Gopher is alert.

One of two things will now happen. Either your inner Gopher wins and you go for it, diverting valuable time and attention from what you intended doing, or you suppress your inner Gopher and feel bad about it. The constant struggle leaves you feeling guilty and a fraud.

If you don't feel like saying '*Absolutely, YES*' to a request, an opportunity or a choice, then you will always be better off to say a clear '*NO*'. Make a Noble Objection and move on.

The overchoice problem

At the start of Chapter 1, we encountered the term '*overchoice*', which was coined by Alvin Toffler in 1970, to mean the excessive number of choices we have. Too many choices for things to buy, projects to take on or things to do, introduces a chain of problems.

The first is how to make an '*informed choice*'. How can you get information about all of your choices, to make a well-informed decision about which to choose? Now you start worrying about '*mistakes*'. The more choices you have, the more complex your decision is. The more complex your decision is, the more mistakes you could make. Finally, you succumb to '*fear*'. You may have the information you need to make your choice, or you may not. But how to use it. Too much choice leaves you with the fear that you will get it wrong.

Choice is a good thing. We can all agree on that. But, ironically, too much of a good thing… If we have too much choice, it leaves us more stressed, less able to decide and, crucially, with less of a sense of well-being. Maybe we were better off with a few good TV stations than in the current multi-channel world.

Solving the overchoice problem

The way most of us deal with the huge array of TV channels available to us is to ignore most of them and select from among a small number of channels that often have programmes of interest to us. We know that there *might* be something good on Channel 9635, but we put it out of our mind.

As long as you find something good enough to entertain you, you don't worry too much about what you are missing. Psychologists call this strategy '***satisficing***'. This is when you make a decision that satisfies sufficient conditions and you stop your search for an optimum option.

The alternative strategy is '***maximising***': looking for the very best option before making a decision. This way you will always see the very best programme on TV at any one time. You may, however, miss the start, because you took so long to review all of the channels.

Maximisers do better in life on most objective, materialistic measures. They take the trouble to buy the best TV, they search exhaustively for the right paint colour and they select carefully the right job. But they are rarely happy. They don't always get it right, so maximisers often feel regret, blame, depression and sometimes even neurosis. And, as a bonus, they can spend a ridiculous amount of time making their decision and still find themselves wondering *'what if…'*.

Maximisers are very good at saying 'YES', but not good at saying 'NO'. Consequently, they always worry about all of those things they said a weak 'no' to, and how those may really have been the right things.

Satisficers don't always get the very best, but they are more often happy with what they do get. They tend to be happier, more optimistic, more satisfied with their lives and, critically, have greater levels of self-esteem and self-confidence.

Satisficers are also good at saying 'YES' to the choice they make, but they are good at saying 'NO', too, to all of the options they have rejected. When they want a new TV, they choose three or four to look at carefully and pick the best. It never occurs to them to worry about the three or four hundred they didn't consider. While they are sitting enjoying Channel 8143 with their family, the maximiser is still wading through their two hundredth consumer report.

How to be more of a satisficer

One of the problems with saying 'YES' is that it shuts out other options, and maximisers feel uncomfortable with these 'no's. These become a loss, and fear of a loss can hobble their decision making. The Maximising Gopher focuses on the potential losses inherent in each decision it makes.

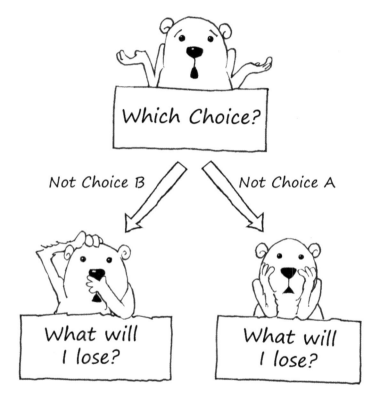

To avoid this, you need to focus on which selection is right, now. Here is a seven-step process to help you focus on your options positively and become better at satisficing.

Decision-making process

1 Decide what success will look like. Set objectives for what you want or criteria for 'good enough', or 'done'.

2 Accept that there may be many 'right choices' that satisfy your needs.

3 Draw up a shortlist of options that best appear to meet your needs.

4 Look at each choice and find the main benefits of each. Also look at the main drawbacks of each option.

5 Evaluate each option against your objectives or criteria.

6 How do the results of your evaluation feel to you?

7 Embrace one option totally: say 'YES' to that, and put the others into the 'NO' pile.

Having chosen your path, focus on it 100 per cent. Take full responsibility for your decision and know that, if things do not go perfectly (and they often won't), you will be able to figure it out and adjust your road.

Of course, some choices may turn out to be wrong. If one is, then stop and reconsider. We often learn more from our mistakes than we do from our successes, so make a new choice and, when you get the opportunity, reflect on what made your first choice incorrect.

You will be happier and more self-confident when you learn to satisfice more easily: accepting 'good enough' and moving forward without regret. One of the most important aids to this is to avoid any temptation to compare yourself to other people. What often drives us to maximising is not a feeling that we haven't got what we want or need, but a worry that the person next door has more of it than we do. Who cares what my neighbour has? If I have what I want, that should make me very happy.

Decision making

How do you make decisions? Do you sometimes think all of the options through carefully, weighing the pros and cons? Do you like to test out your options by giving them a trial? Are you swayed by compassion and emotion or are you cold and analytical about your decisions? Do you sometimes know what your decision is in an instant, or do you sometimes need to incubate your decision over a long time? Do you sometimes need to talk your decision over with other people and get different perspectives before you finally decide?

Six modes of thinking

All of these modes of thinking are enormously valuable and it would be a fool who would recommend one above all of the others. Each has its place and the important thing is to know when each matters most and what its strengths and weaknesses are.

Head thinking

Head thinking is all about logic and analysis. It is the only method that most of us were taught at school and college. When it comes to decision making, it is robust and reliable as long as you have the thinking tools to help you analyse your options.

If only it were that easy: our brains can let us down! We are prone to make systematic errors due to in-built biases in our thinking processes. And sometimes, the 'right' answer is not the right answer for you. However, when you know about the traps, you can stay alert for them and avoid them.

Heart thinking

Have you ever known the right answer, yet you weren't convinced? You knew that it wasn't right for you – or for the people you care about. Thinking with your compassion is important. Your emotions will help you make a decision you feel good about. How do you feel about your decision? How will it affect other people?

Gut thinking

'*Gut instinct*' is the common term we give to intuition. This is hugely valuable in complex, subtle situations where you cannot analyse all of the data and your emotions are all confused.

In a complex situation, an expert can often 'know' the right answer without understanding 'how' she knows it. What her brain has done is selected the small amount of relevant information from the mass of irrelevant data and formed a judgement on that basis. In his book *Blink* (Allen Lane, 2005), Malcolm Gladwell describes this process as 'thin-slicing' – taking a thin slice of the data. Trust your hunches in contexts where you have deep experience and expertise.

When your experience is thinner and you have less expertise, intuition can let you down, so beware. Often, it is also a good idea to test your intuition out, to demonstrate to yourself and others that you are right.

Test thinking

There is a vital role for experimentation, trial and error, and testing. We often use words, like 'pilot' or 'prototype', to make us sound more confident, but the key is to trust what happens in the real world, rather than ideas, concepts, theory and analysis. If it really matters and if you can do so, test out your decision before you make it. What's the worst thing that can go wrong with an experiment? It is a spectacular disaster! But what would have happened if you'd decided not to run a test?

Slow thinking

Sometimes you need to 'sleep on it'. You need to give your unconscious mind the time and peace to work out the answer for you – to access your emotions, to sort out your intuition, and to get comfortable with a difficult decision.

Team thinking

Two heads are better than one. If you can be shown a different perspective on your decision and hear a different point of view, then you may make a better decision. The secret to making better decisions with a team is to introduce as diverse a group of friends or colleagues as you can. And they don't all have to be experts either. Make sure everyone has the confidence to think independently, by creating an atmosphere where everyone respects and listens to each other. Finally, give everyone unfettered access to all of the information that they want.

Groups really can make far better decisions than individuals, so when it really matters, involve a team.

Tools to help you make choices

This section will introduce you to a range of thinking tools that will help you to make your decisions, and leave you with five top tips.

Tip 1: Look for the vital few things you can choose that have biggest impact

The Pareto Principle

The Pareto Principle, named after Italian economist Vilfredo Pareto, is based on the observation that many types of things follow the same sort of distribution, so there are a small number that reach superlative levels, while many are quite ordinary. There are a few very long rivers and many short ones, a few best-selling books or DVDs and many that sell in small numbers, and there are a few extremely wealthy individuals and many poor ones.

As an economist, Pareto noted that only 20 per cent of Italians at the start of the twentieth century between them owned 80 per cent of the land. Currently, around 20 per cent of the world's population earn 80 per cent of the income.

The 80 per cent of products that account for only 20 per cent of sales has recently been termed the '*long tail*' by journalist and author, Chris Anderson. This gives rise to much overchoice, but also allows people with narrow but deep interests to access a level of choice that is impossible in a world of small bookshops, but becomes easy when online booksellers can have vast warehouses full of products and a list of several million book titles.

Now let's apply the Pareto Principle to making choices. It is likely that a small number of your goals will bring you most of your fulfilment. Given options of many things you could do, a small number of them will make a lot of difference to fulfilling your goals; many of them will make little difference.

Tip 2: The old 'pros and cons' method is still one of the best

Force fields

You have a decision to make. Do you or don't you? This one or that one? Yes or No? Imagine the two options are like giant elasticated bungee cords, each pulling you in the opposite direction. Which one pulls you hardest?

NO   YES

Take a sheet of paper and draw a line down the middle and head each column with 'Yes' and 'No' or 'For' and 'Against' or 'Option A' and 'Option B'. Put all of your thoughts on to this sheet and you will find that it will really help you to make up your mind. A good tip is to create an extra section for anything that occurs to you that is neither one thing nor the other, but is intriguing. These ideas may lead you to an alternative solution.

You can find a worksheet for this exercise at www.theyesnobook.co.uk

Tip 3: Sometimes you know the answer; you just have to let your unconscious mind tell you

Confusion questions

There are four simple questions that will increasingly confuse and confound you at a conscious level. This is good, because sometimes, to make a difficult decision, you need to get your conscious mind out of the way and listen to your unconscious mind.

And, if you happen to have a resilient rational mind that is not easily confused, then coming up with a good answer to each question will still help you with your decision. Are you ready?

Question 1:   What will happen if you do?

Question 2:   What will happen if you don't?

Question 3:   What won't happen if you do?

Question 4:   What won't happen if you don't?

What you will find when you have given these four questions sufficient thought is that a compelling goal, action or choice will become even more compelling to you, while other things will drift into the background. The reason is that these four questions will focus your mind clearly on the consequences of action or inaction.

Tip 4: Taking a pessimistic view can sometimes save you from a costly error

Pre-mortem

This is a technique adapted from an original process developed by Gary Klein. It looks at a decision from the perspective of its outcome. Too often, when something goes wrong, we conduct a post-mortem to find out why. Why not do a pre-mortem to spot what could go wrong in advance? Here's how:

1 Take some time out to relax, somewhere you can do some quiet thinking.

2 Close your eyes and imagine you've made your decision. And now imagine everything has happened that flows from your decision.

3 Now imagine that it has all gone spectacularly wrong. Explore in your mind what might have gone wrong, to create a realistic scenario of failure.

4 Now explore what could have triggered this failure. What mistakes were made? What could have been done differently? What would you need to do to get it right?

5 Now reflect on what you have learned. You may decide that the threat of failure is too great and there is little you could do to avoid it: decision made. Alternatively, you may realise that failure – whilst possible – can be controlled by making the right plans and taking care.

Tip 5: When you use a logical process to decide, you can sometimes hear your heart speaking more loudly at the end

Scores on the doors

There are many scoring techniques to allocate numerical values to a range of options to help you decide which one is best. First, however, you must decide one essential thing: will the scores give you your answer, or merely contribute to your thinking?

Here is the process for scoring a range of options:

1 Identify the most important criteria for making your decision. Three is a good number, but use as many as you need, bearing in mind the Pareto Principle: some criteria will be less important than others.

2 Now allocate each criterion a number of points to weight it by importance – more points for more importance. Perhaps weight each on a scale of one to five points.

3 Now take each option, one at a time. Score Option A against the first criterion. A scale of zero to ten can work well, where zero means it completely fails to meet your needs under this criterion and ten means it meets all your requirements perfectly. Now score it against all of the other criteria, and repeat for each option.

4 Now multiply each score, from Step 3 by the importance weight in Step 2. So, if Option A scored 3/10 for Criterion 1, and Criterion 1 has a weight of 4, then the final, weighted, score for Option A on Criterion 1 is 3 x 4 = 12.

5 Now add all of the weighted scores for each option to give a total score. The option with the highest total score is the superior option.

Consider the example below.

DECIDING WHAT MOVIE TO WATCH TONIGHT

Here, I decide that four DVDs have attracted my attention and I want good acting above all tonight. I also fancy some excitement and I'd like a bit of emotion too.

	Acting	Excitement	Emotion	Total
Weights	4	3	2	
Star Wars	3x4=12	8x3=24	4x2=8	44
The Godfather	7x4=28	7x3=21	6x2=12	61
Casablanca	5x4=20	6x3=18	8x2=16	54
It's a Wonderful Life	6x4=24	4x3=12	10x2=20	56

You can find a worksheet for this exercise at www.theyesnobook.co.uk

Using my Scores on the doors technique, I realise *The Godfather* is the film for me.

Why am I left feeling I'd sort of like to see *It's a Wonderful Life*? Perhaps I misread my mood and I really want an emotional film more than an exciting one.

Criteria for YES or NO

We have looked at some techniques that you can use to decide YES or NO. Before we look at some examples of what to say 'YES' or 'NO' to, let's examine some of the most valuable criteria for making that decision. These are criteria that will serve you well, in a wide range of circumstances.

I believe that your perfect decision will be informed by pragmatism, awareness of consequences, choosing your future, looking for flow, knowing your goals, guided by values, and being truly you. Let's explain these, one at a time.

Informed by pragmatism

Before you make your decision, think through the options you have and the resources available to support you. A decision is only right when you follow up on it positively and seize the initiative. This means you need to know the 'how' as well as the 'what' of your decision.

Practicalities mean plans – and plans have six essential elements.

1 The things to do
… the steps you need to take and the things you need to make.

2 The sequence
… the logical order in which to tackle tasks to stay efficient and miss nothing.

3 The timing
… when to do things, how long they will take, and the deadlines to set.

4 The resources you need
… the assets, materials, people, and money it will take to get things done.

5 Dependencies and constraints
… the links between what you are going to do and other things in your and others' circles of control.

6 Assumptions, uncertainties, risks and issues
… s*** happens! What are you assuming without evidence, what do you not know, what could go wrong, and what is already a problem?

Awareness of consequences

When you think about consequences, there are four constituencies to consider.

Me

How does your decision affect you? Your first constituency is yourself; your very own 'me'. This must be your primary concern, because it will be nobody else's. You cannot expect or require anybody else to take responsibility for you, so start by asking *'How will this decision affect me?'* This doesn't mean that your decision should or will always be led by self-interest, but if you aren't aware of where your interests lie and how your choice will affect them, then your decision will be blinkered.

You

Think about how your decision will affect the other people in your life, who are important to you. For each one, ask yourself: *'How will this decision affect you?'* You are not obliged to take responsibility for the other people in your life – but you may choose to.

Them

You are also not obliged to take responsibility for the great mass of 'them' out there – the people your choices will touch. But again, you may choose to. It is essential to find the right balance for yourself between selflessness, which can make you feel noble, and selfishness, which can prevent you from feeling like an unrecognised martyr.

The universe

OK, you don't owe the universe anything, but it is wise to also think about what is 'right' in whatever terms that word suggests to you. I don't want to moralise and suggest that you must always do what is right: that's up to you. But if you don't even think about right and wrong, then your decision will expose you to the possibility of later regret.

Choosing your future

We take on lots of things, but success in any of them means having the time and energy to devote to mastering the skills we need. This becomes a problem if we take on too many things. We risk becoming a '*Jack or Jane of all things, master of none*'. People are rightly suspicious if you claim expertise in too many areas of endeavour.

Therefore you need to be able to make the decision, from time to time, to give up. To no longer pursue greater skill levels in some arenas, so you can free up the time to pursue them in others. This is difficult, because the investment you have already made feels like a compelling argument to continue. But be aware of the consequences: if you try to do more than you have the time to do, you will fail: you won't achieve what you want and you will quite possibly burn yourself out en route.

Alternatively, when you have decided to pursue one goal, then be prepared for setbacks. They almost certainly will occur from time to time. Because this is what you have chosen, pick yourself up, dust yourself off, and move on. By all means take time to re-evaluate your choices, but the setback itself is not a reason to give up.

Looking for flow

The choices you make will be happiest – all other things being equal – when they support you in using and building on your strengths. When we do something we are good at, to the limit of our skills and experience, and we have a clear goal in mind and the ability to track our progress, we can readily enter what psychologist Mihaly Csikszentmihalyi calls a '***flow state***'. Here we lose all track of time and have a deep sense of satisfaction from what we are doing.

Knowing your goals

In the final section of Chapter 3, we looked at how to discover your goals. Let your choices be led by your knowledge of your goals and also by an understanding of your guilt.

Get to know your typical responses and what sorts of things trigger your inner Gopher to go for guilt-directed decisions that are driven by fear, a need to escape, or by guilt.

When you face a decision, ask yourself:

> *'If I say yes to this:*
> *will this be a guilt-directed yes, or a*
> *goal-directed YES?'*

Guided by values

Your values direct your choices: they are the things that are most important to you in life. The challenge for us all is to re-evaluate our values from time to time, so that we don't find ourselves making decisions driven by values that are out of date.

Most people acquire their values early in life and never challenge them. They therefore live lives directed by decisions based on inherited values that really belonged to their parents or caregivers, their families and friends, their schools and religious institutions, their society and cultural background. None of these did you choose for yourself.

These inherited values are, at best, an approximation of your 'true' values. There is nothing wrong with sharing your values with your family, your teachers and your faith leaders; what is wrong is doing so when these are values you might reject if you were to examine them for yourself.

When you understand and choose your own values, and make choices that accord with them, this is called integrity. When, however, you make choices that clash with your true values, you will find yourself stressed and dispirited.

Being truly you

The gold standard of personal decision making takes all of these factors into consideration and synthesises them into a decision that is 'truly you'. Now, your decisions are led by a deep knowledge of who you are, and also what you believe is your own route to fulfilment. When you know that, saying 'NO' and saying 'YES' become easy. And so does knowing when to say which.

YES or NO to...

An opportunity missed will often cause far more regret than an opportunity taken that then fails. What this means is learning to say 'NO' more readily to the safe options, so that you can say 'YES' to the opportunities.

Say 'YES'

Say 'YES' when...

- it needs to be done
- it is worth doing
- it leaves time for things you love
- you are fully able
- it will stretch you and teach you
- it excites you
- it contributes to your goals, your desires and your passions
- it will help you build and maintain relationships you value
- it is something to take pride in
- you will learn from it
- it opens up new opportunities, new possibilities, new hope
- your head says yes, your gut agrees, and your heart is convinced.

Say 'YES' to...

- caring about service
- the details – when they matter
- going to the doctor, the dentist, the optician
- fruit, vegetables and a healthy diet
- an early night
- a walk and some exercise

- time out with friends
- being honest
- reading something new
- facing down your fears
- starting the hobby you have always fancied
- courtesy
- a holiday
- saying 'thank you'
- saying 'I love you'
- tidying your work space
- making time for your family
- asking for what you want (if you don't ask…).

Say 'NO'

Say 'NO' when…

- the compromise is too great
- the principle is too important
- the purpose is unclear
- the evidence is lacking
- your motivation would be fear
- things have not worked – and, realistically, never will
- you've already tried the same thing, and failed
- it isn't truly you.

Say 'NO' to...

- a bad habit
- working on holiday
- answering the phone at dinner
- simplistic solutions to complex problems
- despair
- guilt
- doing a job you don't value
- blame and recrimination
- substandard, second rate, not good enough
- losing focus
- dissipating your energy
- compromising your principles
- the petty and the trivial
- a report that creates no action
- regret.

Did you know that 'Non, Je Ne Regrette Rien' by Edith Piaf is the most requested popular song over the first 70 years of the BBC's *Desert Island Discs*?

What about relationships?

'Should I stay or should I go?' is one of the most widely asked questions in relationships – whether they are waning romantic relationships, friendships going sour, business relationships that are no longer productive, or even customer–supplier relationships that are no longer commercially adroit.

Before we look at the YES/NO indicators, let's examine five rules of how.

The five rules of how to manage relationship decisions

Rule 1: **Don't act on a whim, out of spite, when you are angry, or when you are depressed**

Precipitant action without careful – and objective – thought and an examination of what is really going on will rarely be wise and mostly lead to regret... even when you made the right decision.

Rule 2: **Don't let it fester**

If you hide away and hope the problem will go away, it will probably get bigger. Think it through, make a decision, come up with a plan, and tackle the problem.

Rule 3: **Try to get an objective assessment of your behaviours and theirs**

A tendency to blame the other person for their faults overrides a fair assessment of your own. Indeed, quite often we project our own failings on to the people around us, blaming them for our own faults.

Rule 4: **Take responsibility for the issues**

When you start to confront someone, any sentence that starts with '*You...*' is leading the dialogue downwards. If what I do annoys you, tell me your issue. I may be prepared to stop doing it, but I may have been wholly entitled to do it.

Rule 5:   If you have bad news to break, break it up front

Tip-toeing around the topic will do neither of you any favours. Say what you need to say, then give a silence in which the other person can process what you have said and respond in their own way. Listen to their response, without interruption.

THE YES/NO INDICATORS

'Should I stay or should I go?'

Should you stay in your romantic relationship? Should you stick with a boss or a job that is no longer quite right? Should you maintain contact with a friend who is treating you badly? How many of the YES/N.O. indicators for 'Should I stay?' can you tick?

Yes, you should stay if...

☐ you find the things they say challenging, but interesting

☐ you are optimistic about the future of your relationship

☐ when they struggle, you feel sympathy and want to help

☐ they tend to make you feel good about yourself

☐ you find yourself proud of their achievements

☐ petty arguments resolve quickly

☐ in the give and take of your relationship, the give and take seems to balance out over time

☐ when they interrupt you, you usually want to give them your attention straight away

☐ you can't help wanting to be with them.

No, you should go if...

☐ you are most often critical of things they say

☐ you feel a sense of hopelessness and despair when you think ahead

☐ when they struggle, you feel a sense of schadenfreude at their plight, or frustration at their foolishness, or guilty that you should fix their problems

☐ they tend to bring out the worst in you

☐ you find yourself criticising them to close friends or strangers

☐ petty arguments blow up and last for hours... or days

☐ in the give and take of your relationship, the give and take seems unbalanced

☐ when they interrupt you, you usually want to just ignore them

☐ there's nothing much left to attract you to them.

Yes/No in an instant

'Yes' and 'No' are weak: 'YES' and 'NO' are strong. Know what you want and embrace it fully: otherwise, reject it firmly. Faced with too many options, adopt a satisficing strategy and focus on the benefits of the YES option, rather than what you lose by saying 'NO'.

Combine head, heart, gut, test, slow and team thinking to make your decisions, and use the thinking tools that are available to you. The criteria for choosing YES or NO start with pure pragmatism and end with being truly you.

Yes/No: Faced with overchoice, will you always try to maximise your gain, and thus end up less happy?

Yes/No: Will you combine different thinking modes and tools when making your choices?

Yes/No: Have you reviewed your own criteria for YES or NO?

Yes/No: Are you ready to learn to say 'YES' with style?

CHAPTER 5

How to say 'YES'

So far, much of this book has been about the need to say 'NO'. So it may seem strange to find a chapter about how to say 'yes'. But since you are going to say it many times in your life, and very often you are going to mean it too, it is important to learn how to say it well.

How you say 'yes' matters

How you say 'yes' matters. It will have a big impact on how people perceive you. Think about how differently you would feel, having asked me to give you some help with something that is really important to you if, on the one hand, I reply with a grudging:

> *'Yeah... allright'.*

Or, on the other hand, I respond with a committed:

> *'Yes, I will'.*

'*Yeah… alright*' or '*If I must*' sound churlish. Yet, if I am going to offer you my help, the resulting work that I have to do will be just the same, whether my response is weak and resentful or strong and positive. So I may as well use the better words.

There is a spectrum of ways you can say 'yes':

> ***If I must   I suppose so***
> ***Alright   OK   Yup   Yes   YES***

The one you choose matters. If yes is what you mean, then don't just say it in a feeble way: give it a 100 per cent committed 'YES'.

If you are not totally committed, say 'NO'. This will leave you with the time and energy to choose what to really embrace and say 'Absolutely, definitely, positively YES!'

YES is an opportunity

YES gives you a chance to make a difference. So, whilst it is important to use it with care, to avoid taking on inappropriate and unwanted commitments, you may want to look for opportunities to use it where you can have a positive impact.

In these cases, use YES on your own terms. Rather than say 'NO', for example, could you say '*YES, if…*'.

YES if...

'YES if...' creates the opportunity for me to transform my request from something you want to say 'NO' to, to something you can readily say 'YES' to. If you look back at the criteria for YES or NO that we listed in Chapter 4, *'YES if...'* allows you to take a request that does not fulfil those criteria and offer me the chance to reframe what I ask you, so I can meet your criteria.

'YES if...' can set conditions like timing, place, the resources you make available, the way I do something and even what is in it for me or for other people. You can even use it as a way to change the request completely.

> *'Will you help us to gather evidence to support dismissing Peter?'*
>
> *'Yes, if you allow me to work with Peter to allow him first to show that he can do a good job.'*

This exchange is substantially a real one in which I was able to change an unpleasant formal personnel task into a powerful learning experience for Peter and myself and, in so doing, improve both of our careers.

Saying 'YES' is the start

Saying the word 'YES' is, perhaps, the easy part. You also need to deliver on the commitment it creates. Anything less will damage your reputation and the relationships that go with it. We've already learned that this is why it is so important to be able to say 'NO'.

If anything, it is better to say YES to less and to leave yourself the possibility that you will be able to deliver more than you promised. That is the way to delight and impress people.

So how can you create the conditions to fulfil the promise of your 'YES'? We'll take a look, in Chapter 8, at how to plan for YES, but in this section, I will show you five ways to kick start your efforts.

Make it right

The first step is to make sure that you are happy with your decision to say 'YES' in the first place. Once you have said 'YES', there is no benefit in asking yourself '*What if?*' and looking at the choices you did not make. Instead, focus on the positive consequences of the choice you did make. Now take responsibility for your decision:

> *'If it's to be, it's down to me.'*

Make it fun

How you describe the task to yourself can have a huge effect on your performance levels. Researchers have found that habitual underachievers in school can outperform the best students when a task is described as 'fun'. When tasks were framed as a test of ability, the usual high achievers did best. When the same tasks were cast as a 'fun' activity, the low achievers performed better and, indeed, outperformed the high achievers.

Create a mindset that saying 'YES' to something means it is something you can enjoy doing. Look for the pleasures along the way – even in the most demanding activities.

Make it urgent

A sense of urgency can give you a real head start into a task. For many people, their favourite technique is to delay starting, until there is genuine urgency. However, even when this works for you, it can make the people around you anxious.

A better approach is to mentally picture the deadline looming and to concentrate on the need to take the first step immediately, to bring the task under control. Once you have done that, you will find it easier to tackle the next step, and so on. Never underestimate the power of momentum to drive human behaviour.

Make it personal

Perhaps the strongest motivator for anyone is to know *'What's in it for me?'* When you see your commitments as a reflection of who you are and your personal reputation, then meeting them becomes more than just an obligation to someone else. Rather, it is a matter of integrity.

Make it flow

In the last chapter, we saw how the opportunity to do things that help you develop your strengths and put you into a *'**flow state**'* is a useful criterion for deciding 'YES' or 'NO'. Once you have decided 'YES', you can often transform whatever task you have committed to into a flow task.

Mihaly Csikszentmihalyi, set out three conditions to create a flow state.

1 **You must know precisely what your goal is, in doing the task:** So, having said 'YES', set yourself a very clear completion criterion and quality standard for what you are going to do and how well you are going to do it.

2 **The task must stretch you to the limit of your capability:** Set yourself a goal that will stretch you, so that it is not easy. Neither, however, must it be alarmingly challenging. Too easy, and you will be bored; too difficult, and you will get stressed. Ideally, it must be demanding enough to take your whole concentration and, in so doing, when you complete the task you will have learned and improved your skills.

3 **You must constantly monitor your performance levels:** So decide what measures will indicate your progress and how well you are doing as you proceed.

Saying 'YES' and doing it now

Procrastination is often seen as a bad thing. In fact, it can be a force for good, as we will see in Chapter 7. However, if procrastination is merely about wasting your time and avoiding doing what you have committed to do, it serves no purpose at all.

Purposeless procrastination

The definition of '*purposeless procrastination*' is this:

> *'Purposeless procrastination is putting
> something off for no good reason,
> and with no incidental benefit.'*

It is easy to say 'YES' and dive straight into a pleasant, goal-directed task. The challenge is to say 'YES' and dive into the unpleasant, unappealing, difficult things that may well take you towards your goals, but you'd rather someone else would do for you, or that you could at least leave until later.

For example, you want a lovely, clean, properly functioning home… and the drains are blocked. You know you need to roll up your sleeve, lie on the floor, and put your arm in, up to your shoulder. It has to be done, but there are other things you'd rather do. Been there, done that. In my case, the promise to myself of a chocolate bar as a reward was a big help.

Another type of purposeless procrastination occurs when a goal-directed and a desire-directed opportunity compete for your attention and time. You could work on making that dress, or building a playhouse for your children, but you also notice one of your favourite films is on television in five minutes. That gives you enough time to make a cup of tea. While you are making it, think through: *'How much pleasure will you really get watching the film, compared to the satisfaction of completing a worthwhile project?'*

The reason why we procrastinate

In each case, the temptation to procrastinate is driven by a focus on the immediate sense of effort or even nastiness of doing what you need to do, compared with the relative pleasure of doing something else. You do not consider the greater, but deferred, pleasure of fulfilling your 'YES'. It's a bit like standing behind a small mound of earth and not wanting to climb over it, without realising that when you do, you will have a magnificent view.

This is your '**Gopher Mound**' – it prevents you going for the thing that matters, because the immediate challenge intimidates you.

Your Gopher Mound could represent the time commitment, your sense of the difficulty of the task, a steep learning curve, your fear of failure, your frustration with past attempts, the challenge of meeting your own high standards, or your depleted self-confidence. Whatever it is, you need to raise yourself up, just a little bit, to see what lies beyond.

Procrastination to motivation

The perfect way to deal with your purposeless procrastination is to create in yourself a feeling of pent-up desire to get on with the task. Here is a ten-step process. When you find yourself procrastinating, open this page up and work through these ten steps.

Procrastination buster

1 **You know what to do**: Review what needs to be done and decide what the first step will be.

2 **And you want it done, don't you?**: Think about the reason why you said YES in the first place.

3 **In fact, you can't wait for it to be done**: Consider what you will get when you have finished, and how good that will feel.

4 **And you know what it's like to be impatient, don't you?**: Remember a time when you were desperately impatient to get something done. What did it feel like?

5 **And when you're impatient, you just have to get it done**: Focus on what is really important, so that you know that this task absolutely deserves all of your attention now.

6 **And then, you are right on the verge**: When you want to get something done it pays to choose just the right moment, when you are absolutely ready to do it.

7 **You feel you just have to start soon**: Take on one small component of the task to get you started and build momentum.

▶

---

8 In fact, you can't hold back: Feel how uncomfortable it is to not start it, knowing how important it is that you get it done.

9 You've got to do it now: You made a promise to someone. If you don't keep that promise, how will you feel?

10 You are motivated!: Get started and you are on your way to celebrating the success of achieving it.

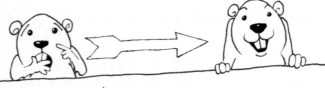

- ○ You know what to do
- ○ And you want it done, don't you?
- ○ In fact, you can't wait for it to be done
- ○ And you know what it's like to be impatient, don't you?
- ○ And when you're impatient, you just have to get it done
- ○ And then, you are right on the verge
- ○ You feel you just have to start soon
- ○ In fact, you can't hold back
- ○ You've got to do it now
- ○ **You are motivated!**

Top techniques for procrastinators

Typical procrastinators need to know that getting on with it is not so bad after all. If you are a frequent flyer with procrastination airways, then you may want to try some of the following cures.

Advertise your promise

More than just saying 'YES', publicise your commitment widely. This way, the discomfort of failure will increase, putting more pressure on you to get on with it. Better still, make a commitment to when you will get started:

> *'YES, I will do that. I will get started on it at 3 p.m. and let you know how I am getting on at the end of the day.'*

Time-box your activity

If the task is too big and intimidating, set yourself a smaller one. Determine a useful part to get done in just 20 minutes and call it Task 1. Now create a series of tasks: 2, 3, 4… each of the same length. Whilst putting off the whole job, dive into Task 1 with gusto. Get it done then take a five-minute break. Now do Task 2. And so on.

Rewards

If the big reward is too far off, promise yourself intermediate rewards for doing the each part of the job. Nothing is as motivating as acknowledging our own success, and a small reward is an explicit way to do that.

First draft

One of the common reasons for procrastination is a sense of perfectionism: some procrastinators don't want to start because they can't see their way through to a perfect end product. So instead of setting yourself up to do the job, set yourself the task of producing a rough draft, with all of the main elements in place. When you have done that, your perfectionism will become your ally by driving you to tidy up the draft.

Objective observer

Another reason why some people put things off is because they tried and failed. Maybe they tried and failed several times. Frustration can motivate some of us to try different approaches again and again, until we get a solution. Others come to a point where it causes them to freeze. If this is your reason for procrastinating then you need outside help: a friend or colleague who can be objective and suggest some alternative routes to take.

Remove distractions

Distractions are not a reason to procrastinate, but they do give you both a means and an excuse. One of the best reasons to ensure your workspace is clear and tidy is that it removes physical and visual distractions. If you are one of the 20 per cent of the population who view themselves as chronic procrastinators, a Spartan work environment will help you a lot. If your work is computer-based, only open up the applications you need to do the job you are working on. Unless you need your e-mails, close them down. Unless web access is essential, shut down your browser.

Yes/No in an instant

Don't say a feeble 'yes' when you can shout an enthusiastic 'YES'. Make it your opportunity to make a difference and make sure you deliver on the promise it makes. Purposeless procrastination has many causes, but it's time to knock it on the head: where's your inner Gopher when you need it?

Yes/No: Will you say 'yes' next time, or will you say 'YES'?

Yes/No: Will you deliver on your 'YES'?

Yes/No: Will you put off procrastination and get on with it now?

Yes/No: Are you ready to confront the psychology of NO?

PART THREE

Choosing NO

CHAPTER 6

The psychology of NO

No is a pretty simple word: in most languages, it is one of the shortest:

no – non – na – ne – nee – ni – nie – nein – nem – nej – net – nu – nao – aon – ei – eki – ikke – di – dim – jo

So you might think it is also one of the easiest to say. But far from it. Most of us actually find it very hard to say 'no', even when we know we should.

Saying 'no' does not just free up time, it releases a greater sense of control over your life which in turn gives you more self-confidence and self-esteem. It will enhance people's respect for you as you shift your reputation from a yes-to-everything doormat to a careful thinker and reliable contributor.

There are many good reasons to overcome the barriers to saying 'no', but first, you need to understand what those barriers are.

Why NO feels so difficult

There are many separate reasons why saying 'no' feels difficult. For many of us, several of those reasons will be compounded in any one situation, making 'no' feel particularly difficult. Let's start by identifying the basic problems, before we move on to understanding the psychology that underlies them.

Basic problems

We can divide the reasons why saying 'no' feels difficult into four basic problems that we may have with it. You could be worried about any – or all – of the following:

1 the response you might get from the person you say 'no' to

2 what might happen as a result of saying 'no'

3 how you might look to other people if you say 'no'

4 how you might feel if you say 'no'.

We will go through these four, one at a time.

Their response

When your principal concern is how you anticipate the other person will respond, and this is stopping you from saying 'no', you are essentially reading their mind. Since mind-reading is impossible, what you are actually doing is believing you know what they will think. Most often, you are projecting your fears and what you might think on to them. Here are some typical mind-reads.

Offence: They will be offended by my saying 'no'

This mind-read suggests that you think there is something wrong with saying 'no' – otherwise, no offence could be given.

Truth: There is nothing wrong with saying 'no'.

Hurt: If I say 'no', it will hurt their feelings

As well as assuming that the other person has somewhat fragile feelings, this mind-read assumes the other person will take your 'no' personally.

Truth: Most people are not as fragile as you fear.

Dislike: They will dislike me if I say 'no'

Here, you are assuming the other person has such fickle allegiances that one 'no' will create real enmity. In a work context, this mind-read can cast your 'no' as a CLM: a 'career-limiting move'.

Truth: If they respect you, then one appropriate 'no' won't turn like to dislike or respect to disdain.

Disappointment: They will feel let down if I say 'no'

When this is your mind-read, you are really projecting your belief that you are the only person who can help, assuming more power for your 'no' than the other person may really perceive.

Truth: Most times, they will have alternative options, even if you are their first choice.

There are two fundamental problems with mind-reading:

1 **Very often, it will be wrong:** You can't read my mind, so any mind-read is a fabrication of *your* mind. It is based on your assessment of me, the situation and how the two interact. Unfortunately, it is also contaminated by your fears, your prejudices and your faulty thinking.

2 **My emotions are not your problem:** Even if I take offence, get upset or am disappointed, these are my emotions, not yours. You do not have to take responsibility for how I feel: your responsibility is for how you act. Saying 'no' respectfully and for a good reason is perfectly responsible. Of course, if your reasons for saying 'no' are capricious or through laziness, then it isn't just me you have let down, and you don't need to read my mind to know it's wrong: you feel bad because you should!

What might happen

Whatever you do will have consequences. Worrying about what might happen if you say 'no' is fundamentally a fear of those consequences. To make this a reasonable fear, you need at least to consider equally all of the consequences of saying 'yes'. However, because saying 'yes' is the easy, expected, default position, we tend to put this out of our mind. Some of the most common fears are explored below.

Argument, confrontation and conflict

Most of us fear conflict. Saying no immediately creates conflict, it is true. But without conflict, there is no creativity. Without the ability to say 'no', you are making everybody else right, all of the time. Conflict is not, itself, a bad thing. When you maintain respect and listen to each other, conflict can drive you both to better results.

Loss of opportunities

Saying 'yes' can create an obligation in the other person and, knowing that, you fear you will lose the opportunities which flow from their need to reciprocate. However, if you say 'yes' too easily – maybe even defaulting to it and never saying 'no' – then its worth becomes devalued to the point where you cannot expect any reciprocation.

Last chance

'If you say no now, you won't get another chance.' This is one of the most powerful persuaders there is. It latches on to our psychological aversion to loss, our desire for what is scarce, and our fear of failure. It is designed to elicit an automatic response. Whilst sometimes it is true, often this is just a bluff or a rhetorical device. And, even if it is true, objectively, how much should you care that this is your last chance? Don't fall for the automatic 'yes' – evaluate the request first.

How I might look

We all worry about how we look – at heart, we are all narcissistic to one degree or another. If all you care about is your image, however, you will never, ever, be happy, content and fulfilled. So get over it and focus on the substance. Let's examine three common fears about how you might look if you say 'no'.

Nice guy/gal

Ooh, how we shudder when we see or read a dramatic portrayal of someone who really doesn't care if people like them or not. It's worse if we meet someone like that in real life. The need to be seen as a nice or good person is powerful in most of us. But ask yourself, *'Is saying no going to cancel all that is good in me?'* Of course it won't. And if you do it well, you can say 'no' and still have people think how nice you were when you did it.

Looking bad

Nobody wants to look bad – particularly in front of people they like, respect or want to impress. Will saying 'no' make you seem incompetent, or unwilling, or not up to the job? It will if you shy away from all of the important tasks but tackle the trivia. If you do the opposite, and if you can offer solutions when you say 'NO' for a good reason, then maybe people will see you as all the more competent and capable.

Risk-averse

'Scaredy cat' is a particularly pernicious school-yard taunt, but it sticks. The problem is that it is also the cause of serious accidents. Don't confuse prudence with cowardice. Fear is a perfectly reasonable response to real danger. Saying 'no' when the risk is too great is just fine. Let's also remember that there are risks in saying 'no' too, and sometimes that is the brave thing to do.

How I might feel

As we have worked our way through the basic problems with saying 'no', we have dug deeper and deeper into our psychologies. Now we have reached the depths of not saying 'no' because of how you might feel if you do.

At the heart of this is a lack of self-esteem. Saying 'no' does not feel OK. Sometimes, you can only feel good by saying 'yes': *'I am OK if I say yes'*. Saying 'yes' can make you feel good and saying 'no' can make you feel bad. We'll begin with the positive feelings.

Feeling good when you say 'yes'

- **Pride in yes:** Some people take a pride in their willingness and ability to say 'yes'. It almost defines who they are for them. *'I'm the one people come to'* or *'I'm always there for Alex'*.

  If this is you, consider who is now responsible for your happiness and success in life. By all means take pride when you can say 'yes' and deliver, but take all the more pride because you don't have to say 'yes' every time.

- **Want to help:** Other people find it hard to say 'no' because they genuinely want to help. They want to do the task or they want to help the person, out of genuine caring for the problem or compassion for the person. It is admirable.

  If this is you, then think about how you can have the greatest impact on the issues you care about or on the people you challenge. Saying 'yes' to everything will soon

exhaust you. By choosing carefully what you say 'yes' to –
and therefore, sometimes saying 'no' – you can be more
successful in helping.

- **Want to say 'yes':** Finally, some people just want to say
  'yes'. They like the feeling of the positive response it gets
  – it makes them feel liked, and helpful and the people
  around them feel good, too.

  If this is you, you are basically in a state of *'I'm OK if other
  people like me'*. You have mentally devalued yourself
  as much as possible and are now a soft touch for easy
  exploitation. It's time to get up and take control.

Feeling bad when you say 'no'

The negative feelings attached to saying 'no' are powerful,
and drive the most determined inner Gophers.

- **Obligation:** A sense of obligation means that somewhere
  in your mind, you feel you owe the world something in
  exchange for your existence. This is not about recip-
  rocating a favour with a friend or colleague, but the
  deep-seated aversion to saying 'no' to anybody or in any
  situation, because you feel it is your duty and responsibility to say 'yes'.

  When we pick up these feelings of obligation and duty,
  they can extend from a reasonable sense of responsibility
  arising from equity or loyalty, to absurd degrees. Some
  people put themselves out endlessly for someone to
  whom they have long since paid any moral debt and
  well beyond the point where their effort is reciprocated,
  thanked or even acknowledged.

- **Guilt:** Guilt for a misdeed is a good reason to apologise and make amends. But, having done this, it is time to move on. Yet there are people who carry their guilt around with them and become an easy target to all comers by saying 'yes' for no other reason than to assuage a sense of guilt that they have long since paid off.

  Examine your history of misdeeds. Are there any you still feel guilty about? If there are, think through what would be the appropriate way to say sorry and offer recompense. Then do it. Allow yourself to acknowledge that you have discharged your guilt-debt and move on.

- **Fear of rejection:** Have you ever heard this sort of ugly monologue play out in your mind: *'No leads to rejection, rejection leads to isolation, isolation leads to loneliness, loneliness leads to misery. I must say yes'*? If you started to believe any of that, then of course you would never say 'no'.

  But none of the links in the chain is true. Rejection by one person callous or shallow enough to reject you because you made a Noble Objection will not lead inevitably to misery; it may even be a cause for celebration. And rejection is far from inevitable when you say 'NO' for a good reason, and you say it with respect. Acceptance is more likely.

The underlying psychology

What is going on underneath the bonnet when you are finding it hard to say 'no'? A powerful model that will help us to understand this comes from the psychological field of Transactional Analysis (TA) and the study of what are called '***drivers***'.

Recall the four types of Gopher we met in Chapter 1: each one felt either OK or not OK. Psychologist Taibi Kahler discovered sets of behaviours we carry out to help us feel OK; to feel good about ourselves. He grouped these sets of behaviours into five groups and called these groups 'drivers'. Since his research, there is a sixth driver that has been posited. It is far from widely accepted by expert practitioners, but we'll consider it too.

So, we each have a subconscious internal model that says *'I'm OK if I can...'*

- be perfect
- be strong
- please others
- try hard
- hurry up
- be careful (the sixth).

The theory behind drivers is that we pick them up as behaviour patterns in early childhood, possibly as ways to reduce our anxieties about ourselves, and maybe even to cope with injunctions and demands from parents and care-givers. However they arise, most of us can recognise in ourselves a primary driver – or maybe two drivers – that we use most often.

Be perfect

A strong 'be perfect' driver will give you a compulsive need to get everything just right, making it hard to say 'no' to even the little details. Seeing completion, accuracy and compliance as signs of perfection will lead you to say 'yes' when it isn't always necessary. The antidote to a driver to be perfect is to tell yourself that you are good enough as you are and if you want to say 'no', that is OK.

Be strong

The need to tough it out and get on with it – especially in a crisis – can cast 'no' as a sign of weakness for people with powerful 'be strong' driver. The solution is to get in touch with what is most important to you, and then to be open and express what you want in a situation. This will not always be to say 'yes' and knuckle down.

Please others

If you have a lot of friends, but are fearful that you need to work hard to keep them, then you may have a strong 'please others' driver. This will manifest in your need to keep them happy at your expense – leaving you angry and resentful that you can't bring yourself to say 'no' to them. You need to start to please yourself, by knowing what will please you and observing that the people who really care for you will celebrate your ability to go after it.

Try hard

The '*try hard*' driver manifests itself by going for everything but really succeeding at little or nothing. If this is you, you easily get bored and frustrated and revert to something else that you can say 'yes' to instead of focusing on your original commitment. You need to just stick with what is important and do it. Say 'no' to the peripheral stuff and allow yourself to really succeed at something that matters, and then experience how good it feels.

Hurry up

The rush-rush-busy-busy approach to life that is characteristic of the '*hurry up*' driver can leave you exhausted. You don't have time to think things through, so you say 'yes' easily to move on to the next thing. You need to take your time and enjoy the moment. Say 'no' to more things, to give yourself the space to relax and savour the good things.

Be careful

For people who are afraid to lose what they have or to risk failure, the '*be careful*' driver dominates. As a result, they see a threat in every decision they make so prefer to default to the safe option and do what is expected of them and, in so doing, discharge some responsibility, too. When they are asked something, the expectation is that they will accede, so a 'no' answer feels dangerous. You need to take chances sometimes to achieve the fulfilment you want. This doesn't mean being reckless, but it does mean that it is OK to find yourself a little outside your comfort zone.

Guilt

Guilt is at the heart of finding 'no' difficult: feeling guilty about the effects on the other person or about the effects on you. Certainly if your heart says 'yes', then saying 'no' will rightly trigger guilt, but it is an unnecessary emotion when you know that NO is the right answer.

This doesn't mean that there may not be a shade of regret that you can't willingly say 'yes'. It is fine to want to help yet to also know there is something else that is more important. Keep the two things separate. Guilt belongs to circumstances where you do something wrong, beyond your ethical and emotional boundaries.

The surest way to evade feelings of guilt is to ensure that you always act with integrity. Make all of your 'no's a NO: a truly *Noble* Objection.

How to make NO feel easier

Before we consider how to make saying 'no' feel easier, let's ask: do you *always* want it to be easy? Anyone who can say 'no' and feel good about it all of the time may just have a thin streak of callous running through their heart. Some things should be a little difficult.

That said, when it is as important as this, it also needs to be a little easy. If it is too difficult, you won't use your NO often enough and you will end up paying the price. So what are the techniques?

Process

Every decision – every yes or no – has consequences. But making that yes/no decision is your choice, so start by recognising that there is no default position. When you are asked a question, instead of thinking, '*Do I have to say yes or do I have to say no?*', think, '*What do I choose to say?*'

To help you to make your choice, use the **'SCOPE process'**.

- **Stop:** A reflex response is unlikely to be a resourceful response. Take a pause to consider what choice you are going to make.

- **Clarify:** What is the choice in front of you? What are you being asked? What are the potential consequences? The next section will help you think about consequences from different perspectives.

- **Organise:** Sort out your thoughts and make a decision as to whether you will answer yes or no or, rather, YES or NO.

- **Proceed:** Give your answer, clearly, courteously and wholeheartedly. We looked at how to say 'YES' in Chapter 5, and we'll examine how to say 'NO' in Chapter 9.

- **Evaluate:** Periodically assess the outcomes of your choice. It is never too late to make a new choice and do something different. Politicians may fear a 'U-turn', but the rest of us know that if we find ourselves going the wrong way down a one-way street, it is probably the best course of action.

Consequences

View the consequences of your choice to say 'YES' or 'NO' from different perspectives, to help you make a reasoned decision.

- **Alternatives:** If you decide 'NO', what are the alternative uses for your time? If you decide 'YES' what do you have to forego to do it?

- **Time:** When making your choice, it pays to get some emotional distance from your decision. For each option, yes or no, ask yourself, *'What will be the consequences in one hour, one day, one week, one month, one year, one decade, one lifetime?'* This won't give you the answer, but it will give you a different perspective.

- **Person:** Another perspective is to think of the consequences of success and of failure for each yes or no from the perspectives of yourself, your family, your friends, your colleagues, your community. A bad 'yes' can affect many people other than just you.

Change

We are going to work through the techniques for saying 'NO' in Chapter 9, but, here, we will review a powerful psychological method that will help you to feel good about doing it and make it seem easier. You'll need to set aside 10 to 15 minutes to work through these 5 steps in a quiet place, where you won't be disturbed. You may want to have some notepaper and a pencil to jot down your thoughts. You can find a worksheet at www.theyesnobook.co.uk

Five steps to make 'NO' easier

Step 1: The moment of choice

Think about the moment of choice, when you have to respond with a yes or no. Make a note of two or three occasions when you have fallen easily into an uneasy 'yes'. These are times when you did not feel in control and you said 'yes' for no better reason than that it felt easier than saying 'no'.

One at a time, relive those experiences as fully as you can. It may help to close your eyes when you do this. Notice what was said, how you felt, and what went through your mind. Was there a moment when you suddenly felt compelled to say 'yes' against your better judgement? Did you ever think 'no', or was 'yes' completely automatic?

Step 2: Your mental models

What did you think about at the time? To what extent were you in control? What did you believe about the other person or people involved in those events? What did you believe about yourself? Were those beliefs rational, or not? Thinking back, to what extent could you have done something different?

Step 3: Consequences

What happened as a result of what you said or did? How did things change as a consequence? What

▶

opportunities opened up, and what opportunities closed down? How did your beliefs guide you to do something you regretted?

Step 4: Challenge

Now start to challenge your beliefs, one by one. What is the evidence for each belief? What alternative beliefs does the evidence support? What would be the consequences of a different set of beliefs about yourself, other people and the choices you have available to you? How would those alternative beliefs change your actions, world and the outcomes you can achieve?

Step 5: Action

Make a note of the actions you can take, to seize control of a '*yes/no moment*'. What will you do differently? How committed are you to these actions, on a scale of 1 to 10? What would it take to move you even closer to 10? How can you do that, too? When you know what actions you are going to take, write them down in this form:

1 'Will I...'

2 'Will I...'

3 'Will I...'

Yes/No in an instant

No. A small word: a big challenge. There are a lot of reasons why we find it so difficult to say, underpinned by some pretty deep-rooted psychology. Use the SCOPE process, a review of the consequences and a five-step change process to make saying 'NO' feel easier.

Yes/No: Has 'NO' been the hardest word to say?

Yes/No: Is 'NO' starting to feel a little easier?

Yes/No: Are you ready to put 'NO' to work?

CHAPTER 7

Say 'NO' for now

So far, we have said almost nothing about timing. But *when* you do something can matter a lot, so this chapter is about when to say '*YES, now*' and when to say '*NO, not now*'. It is also about how to use the time constructively, when you put things off and procrastinate with a purpose.

Time-critical and time-charmed activities

The term 'time management' is a misnomer: you cannot manage time. It isn't possible. All that you can do is manage how you use the time you have available to you (I give you many, many, strategies and tools in one of my earlier books, *Brilliant Time Management*).

With some activities, you have no discretion about how you use your time – you must do them now. If you don't, you will either not be able to get them done or, if you do, their value will be diminished. These are '***time-critical***' activities. Others are more generous or forgiving to you – you can do them when you choose. And often, if you choose well, you can make it easier or more effective to do them, or you can do them better, by virtue of when you chose to do them. These are '***time-charmed***' activities.

| Time-critical activities | 'Now'
When events choose | 'Not Now'
When you choose | Time-charmed activities |

Time-critical activities

Some activities dictate when they need to get done. When you are faced with an imminent deadline or a crisis, you have to act now. If you don't, all will be lost. Interruptions are also time-critical: you have deal with them when they occur. In all of these cases, events choose the timing.

Some things that are not time-critical in themselves create time-critical activities once you start them. Baking a cake is not time-critical, but when you put a cake in the oven, then taking it out becomes a time-critical task. On a larger scale, once your child is old enough to go to nursery or school, collecting them at the end of the day is time-critical.

Some would say a ringing phone is time-critical. *'Answer me now'*, it says. However, the advent of answerphones and voicemail made phone conversations a time-charmed activity. You can always call back.

Time-critical activities rob you of some of your control and are thus potentially stress-inducing. Because you have no choice about when you do them, you must exert control in other ways.

Choice Number 1: Say 'NO' to it

The first question to ask yourself is whether to do it at all. If it is a guilt-directed activity, then your best option is to make a Noble Objection and decline to do it.

Choice Number 2: Cut it down in size

If you don't ditch it, ask yourself how much time you need to invest in it. If it is an urgent call or a vital meeting, can you conduct it quickly, focusing only on the one issue that makes it time-critical? If it is a report your boss needs in 45 minutes, how can you cut out some unnecessary components while preserving the essential content for the decision at hand?

Choice Number 3: Give it away

Maybe there is someone else who could do it equally well – or even better than you could. Is there someone to whom you could delegate the activity, who has more time available, has more to learn by doing it, or who could find better ways to do it? If there is, it's time to go and talk with them.

Choice Number 4: Say 'YES' and get on with it

The reality of work is that many of your responsibilities will be time-critical. And these are your jobs, and they need to be done in full. So recognise that you will, of course, be faced by time-critical requirements that you can't evade in any way. You said 'yes' to them when you chose your job and signed your contract, so stop whingeing and get on with them. Plan your days so that you have time for them. But don't just say 'yes', say 'YES, now'.

Time-charmed activities

Time-charmed activities are wonderful – you are completely in control. You can do them when you choose and, often, by choosing well, you can do them better or more quickly, or more cheaply.

Often, things that appear time-critical today were time-charmed four weeks ago. But you failed to use the advantage that you had to choose your timing, so now the requirement has crept up on you and, *whoosh*, it's time-critical.

However, it is equally a mistake to automatically tackle a time-charmed task as soon as you become aware of it. That is Gopher behaviour. Instead, when you get a time-charmed request or requirement, log it. You may use an electronic or computer-based organiser, a To Do list in your notebook or on a scrap of paper, or your memory. Whichever it is, save it until your next planning time, and decide when to do it. Your principal strategy for time-charmed activities is the next choice.

Choice Number 5: Schedule it

Scheduling is key to good management of how you use your time to do the things you must or choose to do. Once you have mastered the power of the Noble Objection, no other process will give you as much control of your time.

We will look at planning time and how to schedule time-charmed activities effectively in the next chapter, under *'Planning for YES'*.

For most of us, checking and dealing with e-mails is a time-charmed activity. If you accidentally turn it into a time-critical activity by leaving your e-mail program open or, worse, having it give you an alert on screen, whenever an e-mail arrives, you are giving people control over your time. Instead, open your e-mail program once or twice a day and work through your messages then. You will save a lot of time by not switching from one activity to another constantly throughout the day.

If an activity is both goal-orientated and time-charmed it demands only the best from you: high-quality, focused attention. There are two types of focused attention, which are explored below.

Type 1 focused attention: planned investment

These are scheduled activities for which you have set aside sufficient time to concentrate on doing them well.

Type 2 focused attention: serendipitous displacement

Displacement activities are things you do instead of something else you also 'should' be doing. However, if you take up a displacement activity that is important to you and therefore goal-directed, and the moment is right, you can be highly creative, intensely focused and make great progress. These are therefore moments of good fortune arising from a chance recognition that you can seize your opportunity – serendipity.

The definition of '**serendipitous displacement**' is this:

> *'Serendipitous displacement is doing something instead of what you 'should' be doing because, by good fortune, you realise there will not be a better time to tackle it.'*

Special time

There are some times in your week that are particularly well suited to focused attention, whether Type 1 or Type 2. I call these moments '**special time**'. There are five types of special time.

- **Golden hour:** Most of us have a special time during the day when we are absolutely at our peak of energy and creativity, when work just flows easily. For me, it is the first (early) hour of the day after I've made a cup of tea. For you it may be the last.

- **Prime time:** Prime times are those slots in the day when you know your energy will be high, which you set aside for important or difficult work or other activities.

- **Creative time:** Some people are able to build the conditions they need for peak creativity. Choosing the right time and place for this is important. It may be while you are day-dreaming on the bus, sitting at a café enjoying a bun, or once you've stepped into your shower. Let your thoughts wander and listen to your insights.

- **The next bend:** Set aside an hour – or at least 30 minutes – in your working week to take yourself off quietly to think about what is coming around the next bend. What are you and your colleagues missing when your heads are buried in the time-critical priorities?

- **Focus time:** The gaps between activities – like the 15 minutes before a meeting you've arrived early for – are moments of pure freedom. You have nothing you must do, so you can choose one thing and focus on it totally. These can be very productive moments or, equally, very relaxing.

Time-expired activities

Have you ever been working your way through a backlog of work, or papers, or e-mails, and found a bunch of things for which it is too late? You can't do anything now, they are time-expired. Time-expired activities are wonderful.

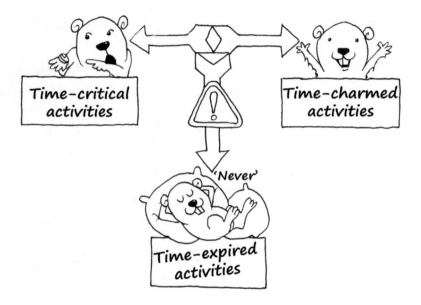

The time to do them is never, the strategy is simple:

Choice Number 6: Ditch it now

There will be no value from doing it; no purpose can be served. Nobody will benefit if you do it and, fabulously, there will be no consequences if you do nothing. So that's what you should do: nothing.

Time-expired activities will feature in the first of our two approaches to saying 'NO' for now, '*purposive procrastination*'.

Purposive procrastination

We first met *purposeless* procrastination in Chapter 3, and tackled it fully in Chapter 5. It is easy to be seduced into thinking that procrastination is a 'bad thing', and it is, if it is purposeless. But not if it is *purposive* – that is, if you put something off with conscious intent.

The definition of '*purposive procrastination*' is this:

> '*Purposive procrastination is putting something off because there will be a better time to tackle it.*'

Purposive means acting with intention and design and your intention with purposive procrastination is to choose the right moment. Choosing the right moment allows for scheduling to take account of, for example:

- efficiencies of doing several like-things together
- effectiveness of doing things when you are prepared, with the right skills, tools, materials, or information
- convenience of doing something when it suits you – because, perhaps, you have cleared something more pressing

- coordination with other activities that need to proceed or succeed it
- respect for the availability of other people who need or want to contribute.

These are all examples of *'Choice Number 5: Schedule it'*, which you could equally label *'put it off until the time is right'*.

There is one other, slightly devious reason for purposive procrastination. You know there are some tasks that, if you put them off, will become time-expired before you get around to doing them. There are many e-mails or requests for help we receive that, if we tackle them now – as if they were time-critical – would chew up our time and cause us angst. Yet, if we consign them to purposive procrastination, we will find that next time we give them our attention it is too late.

A lot of my **'*don't know correspondence*'** goes into this category. I trust my unconscious mind and my intuition to nag me if the seminar details at the bottom of the pile are interesting or important enough to say 'YES' to, but, while I am undecided, they can stay there. When I have a regular clear out, I'll see the date and instantly re-file it in the little round filing cabinet on the floor under my desk.

Choice Number 7: Put it off until the problem goes away

A cowardly alternative to a Noble Objection? Perhaps, but maybe it is a way of consigning a decision to your unconscious mind – a chance to sleep on it for a while.

Purposeful procrastination

Purposeful procrastination is also a good thing, but it differs from purposive procrastination. Purposeful means to do something with a definite purpose in mind.

The definition of '***purposeful procrastination***' is this:

> *'Purposeful procrastination is putting something off so that you can do something else instead.'*

Serendipitous displacement, which we encountered under time-charmed activities, is an example of purposeful procrastination. You spot an opportunity to do something, or the mood seizes you, or you get a flash of inspiration. In that moment, you know following that mood is the best possible use of your time, so you choose to say 'YES' to it and purposefully postpone what you were going to be doing.

Beware false serendipity: is that desire to follow your mood really a unique opportunity or is it just a burst of desire to do something other than your goal-directed activity? As we saw, there is nothing wrong with the hedonism of desire-directed activities, but is the desire really for something insubstantial or inappropriate? How much value does it really have? Is it desire or displacement? Serendipitous or merely slacking?

Purposeful procrastination can also be a planned strategy. You might choose to delay doing something to create time for something else that is more pressing. This is our final choice.

Choice Number 8: Put it off to make space for something else

Creating time for an alternative activity that is either more opportune, more pressing, or more critical is just good basic time management: it is prioritisation.

Yes/No in an instant

What dictates when you do something? If it is events and circumstances, then the activity is time-critical; if it is you, then it is time-charmed. And if it is too late, it is time-expired. You have eight choices for what to do when faced with a request or a requirement.

1 Say 'NO' to it.

2 Cut it down in size.

3 Give it away.

4 Say 'YES' and get on with it.

5 Schedule it (put it off until the time is right).

6 Ditch it now.

7 Put it off until the problem goes away.

8 Put it off to make space for something else.

Yes/No: Will you take control of your time-critical activities?

Yes/No: Will you use purposive procrastination to control the timing of time-charmed activities?

Yes/No: Will you use purposeful procrastination to seize real opportunities to make a difference?

Yes/No: Are you ready to put together everything you have learned so far?

CHAPTER 8

The Yes/No Compass

As we near the end of *The Yes/No Book*, it's time to put much of what we have learned into a simple framework. This is '***The Yes/No Compass***', which will help you chart your direction through life's Yes/No decisions, so you can use your time to your very best advantage. We will look at the four directions on the compass and take a particular interest in the special direction of focused attention.

Finding your direction

In Chapter 3, we met the distinction between goal-directed and guilt-directed activities, and saw that goal-directed activities are the ones to say 'YES' to. These are the things you either must do – so you may as well do them with spirit – or the things you want to do, because they take you towards your goals.

Guilt-directed activities, however, are driven by a sense of 'should' or 'ought'. These are the things you do for other people and through a duty to which you are no longer fully committed. We do them out of fear of the consequences of not doing them rather than out of a true passion and commitment to get them done.

In Chapter 7, we distinguished between time-critical and time-charmed activities. Time-critical activities set their own deadline – you have no choice when to do them and therefore you need to tackle them now. Time-charmed activities allow you to be in charge, and choose when you do them. The best time is rarely now.

We can plot all four types of activity on a single chart, to produce the Yes/No Compass.

On this compass, you can see that the lower half is characterised by time-critical activities – it represents 'Now'. The upper half represents 'Not now'. To the right, we have goal-directed activities, to which we will want to say 'YES'. To the left, are the activities we would prefer to say 'NO' to.

Some activities will not lie on this compass:

- time-expired activities that are no longer of value
- displacement-directed activities that never would have a value because they are about wasting your time
- desire-directed activities that are purely about taking pleasure in the moment.

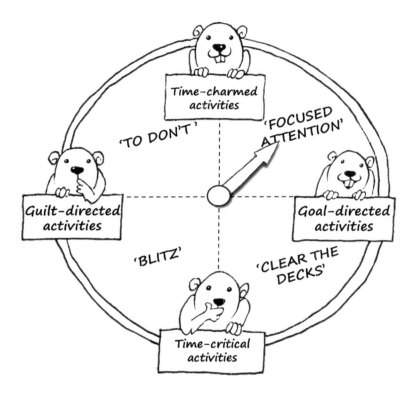

None of these requires a decision. As soon as you think about them, the first two will instantly strike you as deserving a 'no'. If your activity is truly desire-directed, you will have made up your mind already: it's a 'YES'.

Any other activities will lie somewhere else on the compass. They will be partly goal-directed and partly guilt-directed. And they will be somewhat time-critical and somewhat time-charmed. Between the four cardinal directions are four regions. Each has a principal strategy for activities that lie in the zone. Let's examine these one at a time, moving around the compass as we go.

Focused attention

The direction of '***focused attention***' is the special direction. In this direction are activities that will make a real difference, and for which you have the time to plan how you tackle them. You can do them well, efficiently, and at the right time. When you do choose to do them, you can give these tasks focused attention that will allow you to enjoy the process – perhaps getting into a flow state – and complete them to the quality standard that you choose.

The sorts of activities that will attract this focused attention include creative tasks and inventing new ideas, pursuing the opportunities to transform your work or your life, following your passions and moving towards your goals, building and maintaining the relationships that matter to you, and planning and preparing for the next important project.

Clear the decks

You must make time to deal with pressing priorities that are goal-directed and time-critical. Set everything else aside and '***clear the decks***', because these activities are usually needed to meet the deadlines attached to essential projects or are crises that emerge in important parts of your work or life. You have no choice but to tackle them and no option but to do it now. You must be flexible and recognise that all your other '*focused attention*' activities will need to get pushed back, and may themselves become '*clear the decks*' activities if the delay is too great.

How do you keep the amount of time you spend in this region to a minimum? The answer is to ensure that you use your focused attention time well, to ensure that all of your deadline-driven activities are scheduled and are completed well ahead of the deadline. This way only problems and crises that are truly outside of your control will emerge here. As you get better at navigating with your Yes/No Compass, you will find ways to extend your zone of control outwards to help the people around you manage their deadlines and hence reduce the number of crises you need to become involved in.

Blitz

I know that the region labelled '*blitz*' lies on the 'NO' half of the compass. These are time-critical, guilt-driven activities. However, the time-criticality means that often you won't be able to say 'NO' effectively – it will be too late. These sorts of interruptions and ritual activities, like attending a meeting here and answering an e-mail there, can't always easily be turned down without triggering a lot of guilt or fear of the consequences, which substantially outweigh the scope of the task. Sometimes, it is just better to get on and do it.

But do it as quickly and efficiently as possible. Do it to the minimum acceptable standard and give it the minimum time possible. A good way to tackle the little admin-type tasks that accumulate is to blitz them. Set aside a fixed amount of time in your week, or day – say 30 minutes. Make it your mission to get through as many of these tasks as you can in that time. Start with the most pressing and valuable tasks and work on them quickly and with real focus. You will be amazed how much you can do in that half an hour.

For some people it really helps to put on fast music in the background – but it won't work in a shared work space. You may also find that promising yourself a small reward at the end, if you can get it all done, will help. If you are a competitive person, you can set targets and stretch targets for how many things you can clear in your 30 minutes, or for how soon you can finish everything within the maximum time you have allowed yourself.

To Don't

You might feel boxed into a corner with time-critical, guilt-directed activities, but when your activities are guilt-directed and time-charmed, without any deadline, you have plenty of time to take control, and put them in your '*To Don't*' pile. The concept is simple, most of us have a To Do list of things we intend to do sometime, so why not create a list or a pile of things you intend to *not* do?

TO DON'T EXERCISE

Go through your To Do list now. Look for any item that is neither time-critical nor goal-directed. I know that you feel you should do these things but how much difference will they really make? I bet some of them have been hanging around on your To Do list for weeks – maybe longer.

Start a new list. Label the top of a sheet of paper '**To Don't**' and transfer these 'ought to', 'should' and 'maybe' tasks on to your To Don't list and cross them off your To Do list. Well done. You've now cleared down a number of To Do items quickly and efficiently. You will feel a lot less stressed by these items, which only served to keep you feeling guilty that you hadn't done them. They drained you of mental and emotional energy without offering significant opportunities to make your life better.

Now, what to do with your To Don't list? If you are feeling really brave, then screw it up and file it in the little round filing cabinet on the floor, by the door. If you are less courageous and are concerned, you may want to refer to it in a week or two (you won't), then file it in a drawer somewhere. Here, it will be safe, but make sure it isn't a drawer you use often as otherwise, these To Don't items will continue to nag you unnecessarily. ▶

Sometimes you will struggle over whether or not to transfer an item to your To Don't list. The test is simple. If you really don't want to transfer it (but know somehow that you should), are you prepared to take one small step towards completing this task today? If not, transfer it. The worst that can happen is, someday, this task will pop back into your consciousness. You know what? That means it may be time. Then will be the time to put it on your new To Do list and schedule it for some focused time.

Planning for YES

The master process for planning your time is the '**OATS process**'. This is a powerful principle, based on human psychology and the established disciplines of successful project management.

You can do your OATS planning on a daily, weekly, fortnightly or monthly basis. It has only four steps to it.

Outcome

Start off by thinking what outcome or outcomes you would like for the day, week, fortnight or month ahead. What do you want to be different by the end, compared to how things are now? Outcomes should describe meaningful changes that have value to you or to other people. They may take you towards one of your goals or make a contribution to something you have committed to.

Outcomes are worthwhile, and therefore motivating. To give your motivation a further boost, ask yourself:

> *'What will it mean to me when I achieve this outcome?'*

Activities

Next, for each outcome you have set, list all of the activities you need to carry out to achieve the outcome. This may seem like little more than a To Do list, but it is a highly focused To Do list, where every single activity is clearly goal-directed.

Time

The trickiest part of the OATS process is estimating the time that each activity will take. The more you practise this, however, the better you will get at it. The best way to estimate is on the basis of experience – yours if you have it, other people's if you don't. And remember that we are all prone to underestimate how long things will take us to do, so always add plenty of contingency time for underestimates and problems. If you can get a second opinion from someone else on big and important tasks, this would be wise. Not only will their estimate implicitly check your assumptions, but when both of you understand the task equally, you will find that people are more realistic about others' time and efficiency than we are about our own.

Schedule

The most important step of all is to schedule your tasks into your day, your week, your fortnight or your month. The commonest reason why things don't get done is because something else crowds them out. If you have scheduled a particular time-slot to do it, then when someone asks you to help with something else, it is easy to look them in the eye and say:

> *'No. I'd like to help, but I have another commitment.'*

Choose a time to schedule each activity that will allow you to give it the focus and care it needs, and to do it as effectively as possible, using the principle of purposive procrastination that you read about in Chapter 7.

Yes/No in an instant

Use the Yes/No Compass to decide what strategy to apply to any activity. For tasks that merit the all-important *'focused attention'*, use your OATS process to plan them into your day, week, fortnight or month.

Yes/No: Does it require focused attention?

Yes/No: Have you demoted some of your To Do tasks to your new To Don't list yet?

Yes/No: Have you decided when you are going to make your OATS plan?

Yes/No: Are you ready to say NO?

CHAPTER 9

How to say 'NO'

Being able to say 'NO' whenever you choose to, comfortably, requires two characteristics. The first is a thick skin. Saying 'NO' can elicit an adverse reaction, no matter how well you do it. If you do it well, a common reaction is envy: people can be jealous of your ability to say 'NO' effectively.

However, the most important thing to bear in mind is that, while saying 'yes' will make you popular, it will not always win you respect. If you go back to the meaning of NO, a Noble Objection, it will help you to remember this important distinction and make saying 'NO' as comfortable as possible.

The second characteristic you need is a relentless focus on what is important to you. You only have one life, so you need the wisdom to know what you want from it, and the determination to remain goal-directed in your choices.

To support your willingness and determination, this chapter offers you techniques to help you say 'NO' well.

How to say 'NO' with grace

The perfect outcome to saying 'NO' would be that both you and the person you say it to feel more than comfortable with your choice; you both feel good about it. There is no shadow of bitterness from the other person and you feel no grain of remorse. How can you achieve that? In a moment, we'll look at a four-step process you can follow, but before we do, I'd like you to understand the essential underlying principle. I've discussed it before, particularly when we examined the types of Gopher and the psychology of NO. That principle is '***respect***'.

Nature of assertiveness

Saying 'NO' is the ultimate in assertiveness: you are asserting your right to choose how you use your time. And assertiveness is founded upon respect. Let's remind ourselves of three behaviour types.

1 **Aggressive behaviour:** Aggressive behaviour is characterised by putting yourself first and demanding that your needs be met – rather than asking and then listening to the response. It focuses on beating the other person, to whom it shows little or no respect.

You may feel that people have no right to ask you to help. It's as if they don't care about what is important to you, so you react aggressively.

2 **Passive behaviour:** When you are passive, you are prepared to subordinate your own legitimate needs and desires to those of others. You are afraid to disagree, find it hard to put your own point of view, and feel guilty about saying 'no'. In doing so, you are showing little or no respect for yourself. Passive behaviour is focused on not getting hurt.

You may feel like you have no right to say 'NO' because other people's needs are more important than yours. You respond with a timid 'yes'.

3 **Assertive behaviour:** Assertive behaviour is confident, collaborative and wholly respectful of yourself and of others. It allows you to say what you think and feel, to be sincere, and to focus on getting the best results by overcoming barriers.

You recognise people's right to make requests of you and you have a clear understanding of what is important to you, so you give a confident 'YES' or 'NO', depending on the circumstances.

Truly assertive behaviour is motivated by honest intention and is mediated by courtesy and openness. Let's look at a four-step process that can achieve this.

Four-step process

The four steps we will discover are:

1 make a robust choice so that your intent is honest

2 confidently and courteously say 'NO'

3 offer a reason for your NO

4 suggest some alternatives, if you are able.

Step 1: Robust choice

Your first response to any request must be to acknowledge it. To not do so is rude, it can cause friction and invites the other person to mind-read that you do not respect them enough to respond. Indeed, in respecting them, you must also acknowledge to yourself that, no matter how inconvenient the request may seem, they do have the right to make it. But so do you have the right to respond as you choose… if it is a genuine request, rather than an instruction or a command.

So you need to decide how to respond. For that, use the SCOPE process that is fully described in Chapter 6:

Stop for a moment

Clarify the request

Organise your thoughts

Proceed with your response

Evaluate the outcomes later

Step 2: Confident NO

A confident NO is polite yet firm. You don't need to be defensive, but if you are genuinely sorry that you cannot say 'YES', then say so. What you must do is take responsibility for your choice by using the word 'I' – '*I am unable to do this...*' or '*I would rather not...*'. If, instead, you seek to blame your NO on someone else, or on circumstances, you will sound weak and will not win the other person's respect. Rather than say, '*My boss has given me work that is more important...*', say, '*I need to prioritise the work my boss has given me.*' Instead of, '*There's so much on my plate at the moment...*', say, '*I have a lot on my plate, so I need to give all my attention to that.*'

Nothing betrays a lack of confidence as clearly as your body language, so ensure that all of the signals you give out are fully aligned. Your voice should be firm and steady, neither too loud (defensive) nor too quiet (passive). Speak slowly and stop at the end of your sentence. Look the person in the eye and give a small shake of your head to reinforce the NO. Stand or sit straight, and position your body square on to the person you are speaking with.

You don't have to be brutal or brusque to be assertive and confident. There are gentler ways, too, which you can use to tone down your NO. For example, you could spell out the circumstances and let the other person come to the conclusion for you: '*I have a lot on my plate, and I need to make sure that it all gets done to a high standard by the end of the week...*'

Gentler still is to make the other person feel what it is like to be you: '*Do you remember that time last month when you were up to your eyes and people kept asking you for help... and how eventually you had to just say no and hunker down?*'

And if those fail, an appeal to either their vanity – '*As you know...*' – or their better natures – '*I'm sure you wouldn't want to ...*' – may well help you out.

Step 3: Powerful 'because'

Of all the things that can soften a NO, nothing does it as powerfully as one word: '***because***'. When we hear the word '***because***' it seems to trigger a response in our brain that says, '*Oh, there's a good reason. That's OK then.*' Experiments by Ellen Langer, Arthur Blank and Benzion Chanowitz in the late 1970s showed that we are more prepared to grant concessions when the request is accompanied by 'because...' – as long as the concession is not too great. So try saying, '*No, I am not able to help you with that, because...*'

Of course, it is important that your 'because' gives a real reason, not an excuse. Clearly, you are a person of the highest integrity and would never use a fake reason. Even if you were prepared to, however, your body language would almost certainly hint at your duplicity. Even if the other person could not pick it up consciously, they could easily be left with an uncomfortable feeling that you are being evasive. That's not respectful and it will not win you the trust or respect you want.

Why does 'because' matter? It matters because you care about the other person. So you can add emphasis to your 'because' by showing your empathy for them and their situation: '*I am sorry I cannot help out this time because of...*' *– even though I know how important it is to you.*'

Be careful: a word as powerful as because is '*but*'. The word 'but' tells the listener that what they have just heard isn't quite right and the truth is coming. So, when you hear, '*I'd love to help out, but....*', you forget the empathy and focus on the 'but'. Instead, try, '*I can't help out this time, but I would love to be able to next time.*'

Step 4: Empowering alternatives

The ultimate approach to softening a NO is to genuinely soften the impact, not just the perception. You can do this by making a helpful suggestion for how the other person could get the help they need: when you could help, what else they could do, who else they could ask. When you give a real alternative alongside your NO, you are demonstrating that you really do care and that you want to help, by investing the time and effort to put some thought into the other person's needs.

Creating an environment for NO

You can make a NO easier to give if you prepare the ground. You can do this in the near, medium and far distance.

Long range: a culture where NO is acceptable

Nothing says NO is OK as much as a track record of YES. But too much YES leads to an expectation that it is your only answer. A culture where NO is acceptable is one where people regularly help each other out and say 'YES' whenever they can – but also say 'NO' whenever they cannot say 'YES'. Let's take a very physical example: an *'open door policy'*.

In the old days of offices for managers and executives, an open door policy was seen as very forward-looking and staff-friendly. It said, *'My door is open; come and ask me questions whenever you need to.'* It was the exact opposite of *'My door is always shut. If you want to come and ask me something, you have to screw up your courage, knock, and wait until I summon you in.'*

Doors have hinges: they open and close. If managers used their doors to indicate their openness to interruption, they could have it open most of the time to indicate that YES is their default position, but close it when they are overloaded with work, to indicate a temporary NO state.

In the world of open-plan offices, this doesn't work. So, I once made a sign for myself, which I put on my desk saying 'It's okay to disturb me.'

Every now and then, I'd put it face down. The first time I did this, one of my team said:

> *'Mike, your sign's fallen over.'*
> *'No it hasn't,'* I replied, *'I turned it over on purpose.'*

Most work environments are busy places and everybody has their job to do. These days, there is no scope for slack, so we must both help each other out and be allowed to get on with our own work sometimes. How you handle this challenge creates an important aspect of your workplace culture.

Middle distance: setting up the conditions for tomorrow's NO

There have been times when I have had meeting after meeting, back-to-back, all day and every day. It's easy to say 'NO' in those circumstances. So when you carve out some time for creative, thinking, personal, relaxing activities, it comes as a relief. *'My diary is clear this morning'*, you think. *'Good, I can get on with something valuable'*.

Then someone comes along and, quite reasonably, asks you if you have an hour to help them out. Reluctantly, thinking of your pristine, blank diary page, you acknowledge that you don't have any commitments. You say 'Yes'.

Wrong

Of course you had a commitment. It was to yourself, but a commitment none the less. So when you determine how you are going to use your time, to pursue goal-directed activities, you must recognise these as commitments and the easiest way to do that is to schedule your time by putting those goal-directed tasks into your diary as formal commitments.

> *'Have you got an hour to help me out with this?'*
> *'No, I am sorry. I am committed.'*

Immediate proximity: making NO seem inevitable

What if you could say 'NO' before someone even asked the question? If you do that, how can they take offence? They didn't ask you, so you couldn't know what they were going to ask, so it is not as if you don't want to help, so they ask someone else.

To do this, you need great antennae. Pick up the hints from body language, listen for conversations in the other room, be aware of what is going on, check the caller ID before you answer the phone.

> *'Hey Jules, good to see you. I was hoping for a chance to chat, but I haven't had a chance to pop over to see you because I have been so busy today... and now I am racing to get all of this done by 5.30, because I simply have to get away on time tonight. Anyway, is there something I can do for you?'*

Now, if you were Jules, how would you rate your chances? *'Oh, nothing much,'* Jules would reply, *'I just thought I'd drop by, but, as you're busy, it can wait.'* Yet, Jules couldn't help but be impressed by my offer to help despite my busy-ness.

Handling manipulative and persistent behaviour

Saying 'NO' gets difficult when the other person decides that, because it is not the answer they want, they will not accept it from you. It is aggressive behaviour, which ranges in severity from persistence through manipulative to outright aggression. We will look at each one in turn.

Persistence

Persistence may not be aggressive in itself, but merely respectful perseverance. However, there will come a point where you have made your response clear, you have re-evaluated it respectfully, and you have reiterated your NO. At this point, persistence becomes disrespectful – effectively asserting that you are wrong, you should feel guilty, or you do not have the right to say NO. This is not, however, a reason for you to stop showing respect.

You need to match their persistence with yours, and gradually escalate your assertiveness.

1 **'NO':** Repeat your original reasons. Don't feel the need to add extra reasons as these would indicate you are unsure of your ground and feel the need to strengthen your defence.

2 'NO': Acknowledge their arguments and stress that your previous answer and reasons hold – without restating your reasons.

3 'I have said NO, and that stands': Flag up your growing impatience calmly and confidently. Say no more. If you can emphasise the NO by slowing it down and allowing a falling intonation, that will give it more weight.

4 'My answer is NO, and that's final': Now add in some body language. A downward movement of your hands, palms down, as you say 'N.O.', and a locking of your gaze onto theirs signals you mean business. If you sense they are about to ask again…

5 'Now, I must be getting on with something else': When you have finished your sentence, break eye contact and turn away. No more rapport. They would have to be socially inept to think they still have a chance.

Manipulation

Manipulation takes the form of tricks to try and get you to say yes. It is foolish really, because if I can get you to say yes against your will, you are going to feel regret – maybe even resentment and there is a good chance it will backfire on me.

Unfortunately, though, most manipulative behaviour is not calculated with any precision, but takes the form of ritualised games in which the requester and you get locked into familiar patterns. Many of us have been playing these games since childhood. Let's examine one.

If it weren't for you...

When you assertively make your Noble Objection, the requester blames you for preventing them from succeeding: '*If it weren't for you...*' You know this is wrong, and you challenge them on this – '*You need to take responsibility for this yourself*' – and suddenly they become sullen or aggressive and accuse you of being aggressive.

There is no way to win this game. In fact, there is no way to win any of these games. The only thing you can do is recognise the manipulation as early as possible, and refuse to play. Below are lots more examples of manipulative games people play.

Manipulative games

How dare you...

Now, the requester takes an aggressive role. You say 'NO' and their response is, '*How dare you... ?*', making you feel pretty small. If you get sucked into this game, you will find yourself either defending your decision or reversing it. A spirited defence will allow the other person to play victim and make you feel even worse. Getting out of this by reversing your decision may make you feel good for a short time, but will put you in their power.

Poor me

A bit like '*If it weren't for you...*', the '*Poor me*' game allows the requester to play the role of a victim, casting you as a villain for doing nothing but asserting

---

▶

your legitimate choice. Again, you could give in to them, making this a successful manipulation, or you could challenge the behaviour giving them a cue to feel even more put-upon, or you could refuse to play and at least stop it escalating.

Blemish

In '*Blemish*', the requester finds fault with you for saying NO: '*You are always like this, you're not supportive. You're just not a team player.*' This makes you feel bad, of course. So again, you feel tempted to either challenge them (this allows them to cast you as aggressor) or try to prove them wrong by capitulating.

Are you starting to see how destructive these games are? One more…

Now I've got you…

The full title of this game betrays the vindictiveness of some of its players: '*Now I've got you, you S.O.B.*' You say 'no', perfectly reasonably and the requester springs their trap: '*Now I've got you. This proves you are…*'. It proves nothing, of course, but once again, if you get dragged into either defence of acquiescence, you'll only make it worse.

Stopping the game

The only way to get out of the game is to stop playing. Declare that you are both stuck in the game, and tell the other person you refuse to play: *'It really does feel to me like we've been here before. We aren't getting anywhere, except frustrating one another. I'd like to take some time out and rethink this and I suggest you do too. We need a fresh start.'*

If they treat this as another move in the game, rather than the well intentioned opt-out it is, then politely decline to play, and leave.

Are you the manipulator?

It isn't only the person asking for a favour or for some help who can initiate these kinds of games. You may find yourself shying away from an open and assertive 'NO' into a manipulative game to support an aggressive 'no'. Here are four examples.

Let me show you

You want to make a firm, assertive NO, but you can't bring yourself to do it, so you try to show them why their request is wrong in the first place: **'Let me show you.'** This can make them feel small, while you lord it over them as the expert.

Instead of playing the game, say 'NO' and then offer them some advice: *'I said NO because I think there is a better solution. Would you like to hear it?'* Remember, if you are being truly respectful, you will allow them to say 'NO' if they choose.

▶

Why don't you…

Rather like *'Let me show you'*, **'Why don't you…'** attempts to take control of the requester, but this time proposes an alternative, without being invited. It deflects the request and saves you from having to make a choice between yes and no.

Yes but…

Whilst it is absolutely reasonable to say 'YES' on your own terms, **'Yes but…'** is really an attempt to manipulate the situation to avoid either a yes or a no. The interesting dynamic that *'Yes but…'* can create is a whole series of inappropriate options that the requester can't accept (because you don't want to create the conditions for a true YES). When you run out of alternatives, they can then turn on you – *'If it weren't for you…'*, for example – and you will be cast as the bad person.

Blemish (again)

We can all play at any of these games and most of us have turned our hand to most of them at some time in our lives. As an illustration of this point, let's replay 'Blemish' from the other direction. Now it is you who find fault with the requester for asking for help in the first place. *'You are always like this, you never do anything yourself. You're always relying on me. It feels like you're sucking me dry.'* This makes them feel bad, of course. But if they felt tempted to either challenge you or try to prove you wrong by withdrawing their request, then they would be perpetuating the game.

Manipulative games are nasty and insidious. But, it gets worse. After persistence and manipulation, comes...

Aggression

You need a book on conflict management to really get to grips with how to handle outright aggression. It tends to start with irritation arising from your NO, and escalate upwards to annoyance, anger and abuse. De-escalating it – without giving in and changing your mind – requires rebuilding respect. You must start the process.

1 While you might deprecate the behaviours that aggression brings out, continue to respect the other person and start to build rapport by empathising with their anger: *'I do understand that you are angry/upset/annoyed...'* Try to use the same word that they use to describe how they are feeling.

2 Next, state your commitment to working together to find a solution – without conceding that you must necessarily change your mind.

3 Then you may be able to explore options and reach agreement.

One tip is to acknowledge their emotion – as you did in the example above – and then to ask them about those emotions, without asking them *'Why?'*:

'Is there a particular reason for you feeling so angry/upset/annoyed?'

This forces them to analyse their emotions, shifting attention from the emotional part of their brain to the logical part. That in itself will reduce the strength of their emotions. The question 'Why?' tends to evoke defensive answers and you are best advised to avoid it.

Ultimately, you have five strategies you could apply to finding a solution.

1 **Make a concession:** Either a YES or a partial yes. Do this if you suspect this is a one-off reaction and the request matters a lot to them – particularly if the relationship is important to you.

2 **Step away:** If the aggression is too great, it isn't worth the risk of further escalation, so step away until they calm down.

3 **Play to win:** Staunchly defend your NO. Use this strategy if you don't have time for anything else and particularly if the relationship is not important enough to work any harder for.

4 **Give and take:** Make a concession, but only in exchange for one in return. This is nothing more than compromise. It gives you both reason to feel like partial winners and protects your relationship.

5 **Going for 'win-win':** Take the time to find a solution that really works for both of you. Use this strategy when the outcome is important to you and so is the relationship. It is the hardest work, but it can yield spectacular results in the form of innovative solutions and greatly enhanced relationships.

When should you change your mind?

Quite simply, as soon as you realise you are wrong, you change your mind straight away, admit your error, say sorry if necessary, and move on. Politicians have an aversion to U-turns, but why? If you are going in the wrong direction, isn't it the best thing to do? The only way to be right all of the time is to admit when you are wrong and change your mind.

Tricks of the trade: top tips from the masters of NO

To end this chapter – and the main part of this book – I'd like to offer you my favourite seven tips from the masters of NO.

> *Top tips from the masters of NO*
>
> **1** If you can't bring yourself to say 'NO', keep your mouth shut. With your mouth shut, you can't say 'yes' and they will probably get the message, saying *'Yeah, I know, you'd like to say yes, but I figured you'd be busy, I'll go and ask someone else…'*
>
> **2** Ask for more information before giving an answer. Or ask for more time: *'Let me think about it. I'll get back to you if I can.'*
>
> **3** *'What's in it for you?'* is the most powerful question. Can they benefit from you saying 'NO'? If there is a benefit, spell it out.

▶

4 Distraction – *'Oh my goodness, is that the time...'* Stalling or evading the question is neither pretty nor assertive, but it can work.

5 Hide from someone you fear will ask for a favour. If you see the number on caller display and you suspect it will be another request for your time, let the phone go to voicemail, or let it ring out. Is this cowardice or discretion? Shakespeare said that *'the better part of valour is discretion.'* Why risk a fight when you don't need to?

6 White lies and lame excuses not only weaken your NO, but they will make you feel bad too. Be honest, even if it means saying, *'No, I don't want to.'*

7 *'No I can't'* feels a little deceitful – you probably could. In fact, if you made it your priority... How about, *'That won't work for me'?* It is honest and also allows you to follow up with, *'... but what would work for me is...'*

Yes/No in an instant

An assertive, confident NO requires respect for both you and the other person. You can make your respectful NO more graceful by giving good reasons and empathising with the consequences of your NO for the requester. Think ahead and create a long-, medium- and short-range environment that supports Noble Objections and deal firmly with manipulative and persistent requests.

Yes/No: Are you ready to go out and say 'NO'?

Yes/No: Are you ready for more? Are you ready for Super-NO?

Super-NO

By now, you should be starting to get pretty good at saying 'YES' or 'NO' at the right time – and really meaning it. You can say 'YES' to goal-directed opportunities and 'NO' to guilt-directed pressures on you. You know how to separate the immediacy of time-critical problems from the control of time-charmed tasks. You are making progress.

- You are better at knowing what you really want.
- You are better at being prepared to say what you really feel.
- You can communicate your needs more respectfully and more effectively.
- You can spot the situations where you need to be careful.
- You can even avoid some of the situations where you need to be careful.
- You can stand up for yourself.
- People are starting to spot that you can stand up for yourself.
- There are fewer situations where you need to be careful.
- People are fine when you say 'NO' and respect you for it.

- People really value it, when you say 'YES'.
- You are starting to get more of what you want.

Mastery

So what is left? What does mastery of Yes/No entail?

To answer these questions, you need to be totally honest with yourself. What are the little things that you still put up with, but you know you would be better off tackling head-on? Tolerance is good, but not when it serves no useful purpose except frustrating your ability to lead the life you want.

TOLERATION EXERCISE

1 Make a list of the things you still put up with at home, among your friends, and at work.

2 For each one, what are the consequences for you of continuing to put up with them?

3 And what would be the consequences of deciding to not put up with them any more – as long as you did it in a respectful way?

4 There is a trade-off. Highlight those items for which the balance says *'No more!'*

5 For each of these, write down the actions you need to take or the conversations you need to have to break the cycle of tolerance. For some, you may need to invest some time and even some money to free yourself of the inconvenience. It will be worth it.

You can find a worksheet for this exercise at
www.theyesnobook.co.uk

Super-NO

Now that you have done the toleration exercise, it is time to take action on the things you will no longer tolerate. From the list, pick your top priority and eliminate it from your life. And don't be afraid to tell people that this is what you are doing. Do so respectfully of course, but when you tell people, not only will they understand your behaviours that result from your change of direction but they will also help you to stay true to your new course.

You may even want to find a buddy to share your whole plan with, who can act as an advisor, a coach or a mentor, to help you through it. The sort of person who can do this well is often called a friend.

Ten commandments

The Alzheimer's Society does a fantastic job in supporting carers of people with dementia. In fact, they do lots of other things extremely well. When a new case comes to their attention, their local branches work hard to find the ways they can best support both the sufferer and their carers. One branch gives out a simple one-page sheet containing 'Ten Commandments for Carers'. Probably others do too.

In trying to source this document, I found it all over the Internet in many forms and variations. No one seems to know where it comes from. But its message is powerful and necessary. And not just for carers.

The Ten Commandments for Caring for Yourself

1. You shall not be perfect, nor even try to be.

2. You shall not try to be all things to all people.

3. You shall leave things undone that do not have to be done.

4. You shall not spread yourself too thin.

5. You shall learn to say 'NO'.

6. You shall schedule time for yourself and your supportive network.

7. You shall switch off regularly and do nothing.

8. You shall be boring, inelegant, untidy and unattractive sometimes.

9. You shall not feel guilty.

10. You shall not be your own worst enemy, but your own best friend.

Saying 'NO' to...

Here are a few tips and thoughts for making a Noble Objection in some particular cases.

Colleagues and customers

Collaboration is a stated value in a large proportion of the organisations and businesses that I have worked for and in over the years. It can therefore cast saying 'no' as a challenge to corporate values. You can therefore feel – or be perceived – as *'not one of us'* or some form of self-serving loner.

It is therefore vital that your objection is noble. Cast your NO in terms of strategic priorities. Make it clear that saying 'NO' is not a refusal to collaborate, but a desire to collaborate and use your time on the *right* things. Be careful to remember that NO is not a licence to just say 'no' to the things you don't *want* to take on. It must be noble.

'The customer is always right.' If only this were true, decisions would be easy. The challenge is to serve your customer or client with respect and to exceed their expectations, even when they are being disrespectful themselves, or totally unrealistic. But some customers are not worth the effort. They bring a lot of hard work and frustration, but never sufficient custom to truly justify it. The response requires courage – and it may not be your decision to make. But sometimes, the right thing to do is to sack unprofitable customers, or those whose disrespect oversteps a critical line. This will allow you to focus on those customers you want, serving them better, offering them more, and building a stronger relationship.

Deals and decisions

There is a school of thought among professional negotiators that your first response to any request for a concession should be 'no'. The apparent value of any concessions you do subsequently make will therefore appear so much the higher. That's just a tactic.

The strategy behind YES or NO in negotiations must encompass a number of key elements and it seems no coincidence that two of the most influential books on the subject of negotiation are Roger Fisher's and William Ury's *'Getting to Yes'* (Houghton Mifflin, 1981) and William Ury's subsequent *Getting Past No* (Business Books, 1991). Here are four essential strategies:

1 *Be able to say 'NO':* This may seem like an odd injunction, but you will only be able to say 'NO' to a bad deal if you know what a good and bad deal look like, and also that you do have alternatives to a bad deal. So Fisher and Ury suggest that you start by identifying your *'best alternative to a negotiated agreement'* (your **BATNA**). If you were not able to reach agreement, what would be the best alternative? Any negotiated settlement that is better than that is worth saying 'YES' to and any that is worse demands a 'NO'.

2 *Say 'YES' or 'NO' for the right reasons:* Don't get hooked on personalities or behaviours when negotiating. You may like or even adore the counterparty – or you may hate or despise them. What is important is what you are negotiating and the deal that is available.

3 *Don't say 'NO' if you can still ask for more:* At the point where you feel you have to say 'NO', you have nothing left to lose. If you don't ask, you won't get. So look for more options and ask for another concession. And make it possible for the other person to grant that concession, by offering them something in return.

4 *Know the value of YES or NO:* Ensure that you are able to robustly measure the value of what you are offered and what you are prepared to give in return. Without this capability, you won't know how close you are to your BATNA – or even on which side of it you lie.

Friends and family

You love them and care about them, and that is what makes it so hard to say 'no' to family and friends. But it also means that it is your family and friends who can most drain you of your time and energy. You will often do more to help the people you love than you will do to help yourself. So this makes them a priority for practising your Noble Objection.

Focus on the balance between your relationship on the one hand and your own needs on the other. Both are, of course, important and you will never want to prioritise one to the exclusion of the other. But you must ensure you create a fair allocation to each.

You may find that it helps to share the challenge of saying 'NO' with the other person, letting them know why it is important to you, yet you find it difficult. It may also help you, if you ask for permission to say 'NO'. The answer you get will tell you a lot about the importance of the request and the respect within your relationship. When you do say 'NO', it is sometimes helpful to give your personal reasons.

Treats and temptations

It is easy to use the word 'discipline', but if it were easy to apply it, then there would be no such thing as temptation. The trick is to decide what is important before temptation comes your way, and to motivate yourself to say NO from two directions.

1 Fear of the consequences of unbridled submission to temptation and the exclusively desire-directed behaviour it will lead to.

2 The draw of what you will get if you engage in only the goal-directed pursuit of what you have chosen as important.

As in all things in life, balance is the key. Succumbing to a little temptation, in a moderate way from time to time, is harmless desire-directed behaviour. Indeed, it can strip some of the power from the temptation. But if you allow yourself to be controlled by it, it will draw you into addictive and compulsive behaviours that will control you, rather than the other way round.

Irrational thinking

Uncritical and irrational thinking will easily lead you to make the wrong decision. Understand some of the thinking-traps that can lead you down the wrong path. Here are five examples.

1 **Causation and correlation:** It is a common mistake to believe that, because two things occur together, or in sequence, one necessarily causes the other. It may be true, or both may be caused by a third thing or, of course, they may represent a coincidence.

2 **Anecdotal evidence:** Anecdotal evidence is persuasive, but always establish two things: first, is there a bias or possibility of flawed perception? Second, how significant is the amount of anecdotal evidence available, in the context of the whole domain?

3 **Irrelevant evidence:** Some evidence is persuasive but irrelevant. Recent dramatic events can affect our judgement, as can the emotional charge around a situation. Do whatever you can to isolate the facts before making a decision.

4 False premise: Sometimes a decision is presented in the form *'since we know* that *is true, what necessarily follows is this.'* This may follow from that, but remember to check for yourself whether *'that'* is indeed true or not.

5 Sunk cost: A common decision error is to look at what you have already invested in a venture: the money, the time and your reputation. If these things guide your decision, it will probably be wrong. Always make your decision on the balance between the required future investment and the benefits it will reap. Past investment (or 'sunk cost') is irrelevant.

Who else needs *The Yes/No Book*?

We all know people who could do with more time, less hassle or a more productive life. Who do you know, who could benefit from *The Yes/No Book*?

Yes/No: Will you recommend it?

Yes/No: Will you buy them their own copy?

Yes/No: Will you lend them yours?

Yes/No: ... Or will you give yours away?

Who else needs
The Yes/No Book?

Also by Mike Clayton

Mike Clayton is author of eight other books to date.

Smart to Wise: The Seven Pillars for True Success,
Marshall Cavendish, 2012

***Brilliant Project Leader: What the Best Project Leaders
Know, Do and Say to Get Results, Every Time,***
Pearson, 2012

***Brilliant Stress Management: How to Manage Stress in
Any Situation,*** Pearson, 2011

***Risk Happens!: Managing Risk and Avoiding Failure in
Business Projects***, Marshall Cavendish, 2011

***Brilliant Time Management: What the Most Productive
People Know, Do and Say***, Pearson, 2011

***Brilliant Influence: What the Most Influential People
Know, Do and Say***, Pearson, 2011

The Handling Resistance Pocketbook,
Management Pocketbooks, 2010

The Management Models Pocketbook,
Management Pocketbooks, 2009

Mike can say 'YES' to your organisation

Mike is a conference speaker and business consultant. He speaks at conferences, team events, workshops and seminars for companies, associations, public authorities and not-for-profit organisations.

Mike's topics include management and leadership, project management and the management of change, wisdom, and personal effectiveness. You can book Mike to talk about Yes/No or another topic at: www.mikeclayton.co.uk or www.theyesnobook.co.uk